The Emoti

The Emotionally Abusive Mindset is written from the heart of a seasoned biblical counselor, Anne Dryburgh. The third book in her *Overcoming Emotional Abuse* series dives deeper into recognizing the mind frame of the abuser and the victim in various relationships. Her insights evoke a depth of discernment coupled with understanding and sympathy for those caught in the destruction of emotional abuse. This book will help pastors and biblical counselors obtain the biblical acumen to recognize abusive relationships and give sound counsel that produces a transformational change in Christ.

Shannon Kay McCoy,
Certified Biblical Counselor,
Biblical Counseling Director, *Valley Center*
Community Church,
Council Member of *Biblical Counseling Coalition*;
Author of *Help! I'm A Slave to Food*

In an engaging and truly readable style, Anne manages to present complex issues in an accessible way. Anne explores what an abusive mindset actually looks like, not just in clear definitions, but through examples and story. The second part of the book is especially helpful, showing that in Christ there is true hope for everyone. But Anne does not leave this hope as some ethereal aim, rather she grounds it in real and practical ideas. As with the other books in this series, it will prove to be a valuable resource for both professionals and non-professionals alike, as well as providing victims – and perpetrators – of abuse a guide as to how to live out a truly godly life.

Simon Marshall,
International Director,
European Christian Mission

For a concise, biblically focused response to emotional abuse, this is your book. Anne Dryburgh aptly presents various expressions of spousal, parent, sibling, disabled, spiritual, and elderly abuse. Then, navigating with biblical skill in a complex arena, she identifies common well-intentioned behavioral and spiritual mistakes and debunks the misuse of Scripture. Based upon the relational, functional, and substantive callings of every believer, which are carefully explained, *The Emotionally Abusive Mindset* champions the choice to honor God rather than yielding to an abuser's desires. This book packs a powerfully hopeful worldview into 100 pages! A helpful tool for abuse survivors and their counselors.

Sue Nicewander Delaney,
MABC, ACBC

Anne has done it again! Her writing is perspicuous, theologically accurate, and practical. If you think you might be being abused by a boyfriend or girlfriend, a spouse, or a spiritual leader this small book may help you confirm or disconfirm your perception. If you are a pastor or counselor wondering if you are dealing with a case of abuse, or if an elder or deacon has an abusive mindset, Anne can come to your rescue.

Howard Eyrich,
MA, ThM, D.Min,
Director of Doctor of Ministry Program,
Birmingham Theological Seminary, **USA**

The Emotionally Abusive Mindset

Also by Anne Dryburgh

The Emotionally Abusive Parent
The Emotionally Abusive Husband

ANNE DRYBURGH

The Emotionally Abusive Mindset

Its Effects and How to
Overcome Them in Christ

Illumine Press

United Kingdom

COPYRIGHT © Anne Dryburgh, 2022

The moral right of the author has been asserted.

A CIP catalogue record for this book is available from the British Library

ISBN: 978-1-7391698-1-7 (paperback)

ISBN: 978-1-7391698-2-4 (e-book)

My heart is full of thankfulness for the countless people who have showed me how to live well. This all the more when confronted almost daily with the darkness of abuse. There are so many of you, I can only limit this to a very few. Thank you to David & Christine, Dave & Jackie, Johnny & Kerry, Barbara, Anna, Joy, Agnes, and Chris, and the countless others who have faithfully prayed for the work for decades. I think too of friends who have been treated in the ways described in this book. My hope and prayer is that you would know the loving restorative grace and comfort of our Lord.

About Anne

ANNE DRYBURGH, PH.D., is a biblical counselor certified by the *Association of Certified Biblical Counselors* (ACBC), *the International Association of Biblical Counselors* (IABC), and *The Addiction Connection*, a collective of biblical counselors and ministries united for the purpose of training and equipping the Body of Christ in biblically helping addicts and their loved ones. She has been a missionary with *Echoes International* in Flemish-speaking Belgium since the 1990s and partners with a number of biblical counseling organizations.

Contents

Foreword

As the Founding Executive Director (now Director at Large) of an international biblical counseling training ministry, *Overseas Instruction in Counseling*, I've been privileged to meet and work with some of God's choice servants all over the world. Anne Dryburgh is one of those people.

I met Anne more than 15 years ago at a biblical counseling conference. Her love for her Lord and for struggling people was immediately evident. And those twin passions had already taken this sweet Scottish woman to plant her ministry roots in Belgium. Anne was already effectively helping women, but her continuing academic training and personal development as a biblical counselor since has extended the impact of her life and teaching.

This book continues – after two previous volumes in the series – the process of broadening Anne's influence through her writing about a critically needed area in counseling, a biblically-based discussion of abuse. Her knowledge of the Scriptures and her decades of experience in ministry make Anne the perfect instrument to convey these life-changing truths.

May God use it for His glory all around the world!

Dr. Wayne A. Vanderwier,
Director at Large,
Overseas Instruction in Counseling
DiscoverOIC.org

Introduction

FRIENDS, FAMILY, AND church members are people who will be there for you, help you grow as a Christian, support you through difficult times, and want the best for you. I know countless people like this and am thankful for each and every one of them. But this is not always the case. Some people are treated in cruel or thoughtless ways by their spouses, carers, siblings, and even spiritual leaders. This is not how life is supposed to be; it is not how Christians should relate to other people.

During the thirty years that I have been involved in discipleship and biblical counseling, my heart has been broken numerous times by hearing about people being treated in abusive ways. The suffering of these people has caused me to take this issue seriously, believing that there must be answers in the Bible for them to trust the Lord in their situation. This led me to write the two previous books in the *Overcoming Emotional Abuse* series. These are entitled, *The Emotionally Abuse Parent: Its Effects and How to Overcome Them in Christ* and, *The Emotionally Abusive Husband: Its Effects and How to Overcome Them in Christ*. This third book seeks to explore the mindset behind emotional abuse and the behaviors involved

1

across a spectrum of relationships. Inevitably some of the material in this book overlaps with the previous two books in the series in respect of what emotional abuse is and what it does.

How this book can help you

This book is a resource which provides insights into what emotional abuse looks like across a range of relationships. It considers how someone with an abusive way of thinking tends to operate and will serve as an encouragement for those who have suffered emotional abuse and those seeking to help them. At the end of each chapter the main points are summarised by relating the story of a typical couple, Mike and Amy, who grew in their understanding of the issues involved and ended up being a great blessing to their church. The book does not cover physical or sexual abuse but is designed to give some key basic information. It would be helpful if other people would take these insights and explore biblical answers for helping them in an in-depth manner. My hope is that this book will help open this discussion.

What this book is not

A word of caution is necessary. Abusive situations are gravely serious and vary enormously. While insights have been suggested in this book, it is not the *definitive* answer about how to help abused people. It touches on subjects that are tremendously complicated, and where time is needed to address these areas in an in-depth manner to be able to effectively help people.

Introduction

Well-intentioned but unwise advice can cause suffering and damage lives. Wisdom and insight are required on a case-by-case basis – there are no standard cut-and-dried answers.

Section I

1. What Am I Doing Here?

BARBARA IS IN her 90s. She tells of how the Lord has made his purpose for her clear, and the way the Spirit has changed her and continues to show her what needs to be changed in her life. She prays for people all over the world and goes out of her way to help others. In times of suffering and loss, she has expressed her trust in the Lord; during difficulties, her spirit has not become bitter. Barbara clearly understands how to live properly. She knows the answer about who she is and what life is about.

Have *you* ever asked yourself some of the deepest questions about your life? Who am I? What does it mean to be human? What is the meaning of my life? How should I live? These are probably the most important questions you could ever ask. You might wonder where you can find answers to such profound questions. Thankfully, you can discover the answers to these questions in the very first book of the Bible.

In Genesis chapter 1, you read about the origins of the universe and why God made human beings. Before going any further, it is important to reflect on that. The fundamental reason why you exist is because of God.

And since God is the reason why you exist, you can look to him for answers about what your purpose in life is.

You can discover his original purpose in Genesis 1:26-28:

> *Then God said, "Let us make man in our image, after our likeness. And let them have dominion over the fish of the sea and over the birds of the heavens and over the livestock and over all the earth and over every creeping thing that creeps on the earth."*
>
> *So God created man in his own image, in the image of God he created him; male and female he created them.*
>
> *And God blessed them. And God said to them, "Be fruitful and multiply and fill the earth and subdue it, and have dominion over the fish of the sea and over the birds of the heavens and over every living thing that moves on the earth."*

God's image bearer

When you read the rest of the chapter, you will see that not only are all people made in God's image, but also that no other aspect of what God made is described in this way. Both the man and the woman were (and are) equal in this regard. Both are equally blessed by God and have the same value and dignity.[1]

The Hebrew word for Adam in the text, which is used to describe both Adam and Eve, describes the whole of humanity, not just the man or men.[2] When you read further in the Bible, you will see this same equality of men and women being made in the image of God.

> *This is the book of the generations of Adam. When God created man, he made him in the likeness of God.*
> *Male and female he created them, and he blessed them and named them Man when they were created* (Genesis 5:1-2).

> *Whoever sheds the blood of man,*
> *by man shall his blood be shed,*
> *for God made man in his own image* (Genesis 9:6).

> *… no human being can tame the tongue…with it we bless our Lord and Father, and with it we curse people who are made in the likeness of God* (James 3:8-9).

What does it mean to be God's image bearer?

So, what does it mean to be made in the image of God? Being made in God's image can be divided into three aspects. These are relational, functional, and substantive:

1. Relational

When you read that first Bible passage above, you discovered that God said, "Let us make man in our image…". In other words, God himself is in relationship. In other places in the Bible, we discover that God is

Father, Son, and Holy Spirit. These are the three persons of the Trinity. Since the three persons of the Godhead are in relationship, you being made in his image includes being made to be in relationship with God and with other people.

2. Functional

You read that both the man and the woman were given the mandate by God to be fruitful, multiply, and rule over creation. They were both given this task to accomplish as creatures made in God's image – they are *not* a description of what it means to be made in that image. Practices in the Ancient Near East (ANE), a term explaining early civilizations in roughly the same area we today call the Middle East, can help us gain insight into a possible explanation of what this means. In the ANE, statues were constructed by kings as a representation of their power and reign in the far-off places of their realm. The statue represented the rule of the king in that entire area. An example of this is in Daniel 3:1 when King Nebuchadnezzar set up a statue of himself on the plain of Dura, in the province of Babylon. This statue represented his reign over this area. Given this practice, we can probably understand the meaning of the man and the woman being made in the image of God in Genesis 1 to include their role as representatives of God's rulership over his creation.[3]

3. Substantive

There is something about us as human beings that reflects God's image, something inherent in how we are made. Aspects of our substance include things like reason, will, and being moral creatures. What does this mean for you as God's image bearer? Since you are made in the image of God, he has made you to be in relationship with other people, to represent him by ruling over creation. You are also made to be like him in your reasoning powers, your will, and your moral capacities.[4]

What went wrong?

You can see in the lives of people around you, and probably in your own life, that something has gone wrong. You can read about this in Genesis 3, where Adam and Eve rebelled against God and did their own thing. All of us have been suffering the consequences since.

Relationally, they blamed each other for what went wrong, resulting in a power struggle between them. Functionally, they would work in pain and sweat, and eventually die. Substantively, they experienced fear and shame and used their reasoning powers to blame the other person, and God.

God's image renewed

Thankfully, our loving God did not leave us in that state. Jesus, the Son of God, became human. The Bible

11

calls him a second Adam (1 Corinthians 15:42-49). Unlike the first Adam who failed, Jesus was perfectly obedient to the Father to the point of death on a cross. His death on the cross paid for the punishment of the first Adam's sin.

> Therefore, just as sin entered the world through one man, and death through sin, and in this way death came to all people, because all sinned–to be sure, sin was in the world before the law was given, but sin is not charged against anyone's account where there is no law. Nevertheless, death reigned from the time of Adam to the time of Moses, even over those who did not sin by breaking a command, as did Adam, who is a pattern of the one to come.
>
> But the gift is not like the trespass. For if the many died by the trespass of the one man, how much more did God's grace and the gift that came by the grace of the one man, Jesus Christ, overflow to the many! Nor can the gift of God be compared with the result of one man's sin: The judgment followed one sin and brought condemnation, but the gift followed many trespasses and brought justification. For if, by the trespass of the one man, death reigned through that one man, how much more will those who receive God's abundant provision of grace and of the gift of righteousness reign in life through the one man, Jesus Christ!
>
> Consequently, just as one trespass resulted in condemnation for all people, so also one righteous

act resulted in justification and life for all people (Romans 5:12-18).

What does this mean for you? If you trust Jesus, you have died *with* him and therefore no longer have to answer for sin. As a believer, you are dead to the power of sin (Romans 6:6). It no longer has a hold over you. Having died to sin and been raised to life in Jesus, you are called to live for righteousness (Romans 6:12-14). You are made righteous, or justified, through Christ and are called a son of God (Galatians 3:26; son here refers equally to female believers – see verse 28). Having been renewed in Christ, you are called to become like him, who is the image of God (Colossians 1:15 & 3:9-11; 2 Corinthians 3:18 & 4:4) and to live according to the moral qualities of the new person in Christ that you now are (Colossians 3:12-17; Ephesians 4:17-32).

As a believer, you have access to God the Father through Christ and are called to become like him in your character, and are personally responsible for doing so. This is your primary calling in life.

> **If you trust Jesus, you have died *with* him and therefore no longer have to answer for sin**

Mike and Amy's story

Mike and Amy had helped people at their church for many years. Recently they were asked to set up a care group.

They had been disturbed to see how badly some people treated others, in ways that would be considered emotionally abusive. Both of them wanted to learn how to be better equipped to support those being hurt. They read their Bibles to find answers to why God made people, what has gone wrong, and what answers God has provided.

They learned that God made all people in his image – to be like him. This includes being in relationship with God and others, working to rule over the earth, and using their faculties like reasoning, using their will, and making moral choices.

They also discovered that things went wrong when people decided not to obey God but to do their own thing instead. Instead of relating to each other the way God wants us to, people often relate in ways that are opposed to him. As they continued reading their Bibles, Mike and Amy were relieved to read about how God wants to restore people. Jesus paid the price for people's rebellion against God and thereby made it possible for them to change and become who God designed them to be.

To better understand emotional abuse and the mindset behind it, Mike and Amy read about it extensively so that they could recognize the ways of thinking and patterns of behaviors that are involved. Knowing that Jesus has given us the answers for all areas of life in the Bible, including what is known as emotional abuse, Mike and Amy spent time thinking about what the Bible says about the mindset behind it, the behaviors involved, and how to help people.

2. Emotional Abuse: What It Is

Josh was raised in the church; Lauren wasn't. They married at a young age. Before they got married, Josh convinced her to sleep with him. During their turbulent marriage, he would prevent Lauren from accessing finances and use their child to make sure she stayed at home and could not work. When he wanted her to do something she did not want to do, he used the Bible to claim it was God's will. One example was going to the local sports bar with him, where she felt uncomfortable around the other men. Josh would insult and demean her, play mind games, and threaten that he would turn the church against her.

Greg would bark orders at the family. If he did not get his own way, he would become angry and not talk to them for long periods of time. Some family members did everything they could to make sure Greg was happy, trying to ensure he would be nice to them and win his love. Others rebelled against his actions. Neither approach helped Greg. He knew who would give him what he wanted, and so would manipulate them get it. He would argue with those who opposed him, knowing his greater strength would win.

One of these men was emotionally abusive, one was extremely selfish. Can you tell which? (Have a think before glancing at the bottom of the page for the answer.)[1]

What is emotional abuse?

When you are trying to understand the nature of emotional abuse, it is helpful to accurately describe and define what you are dealing with. By having a correct understanding of what is going on, you can deal with things in ways that honor the Lord. Having a definition of emotional abuse is crucial, otherwise we run the risk of saying that someone is abusive when in fact they aren't. None of us would want to be guilty of wrongly accusing people.

Here is a suggested definition of emotional abuse:

> … *any non-physical behavior that is designed to control, intimidate, subjugate, punish, or isolate another person resulting in the victim becoming emotionally, behaviorally, and mentally dependent on the abuser.*[5]

As can be seen from the definition, the mindset involves a desire for control over another human

---

[1] Josh was an abusive husband. He behaved in ways described in this chapter to have control over his wife, causing her harm. Greg was a selfish man who tried to control things and people to get his own way. While it caused suffering and harm for his family, he did not control their thinking, time, relationships, finances, and spiritual life. Both are selfish and sinful ways of relating to other people. Both needed help from the church. Only Josh possessed an emotionally abusive mindset.

being. Emotionally abusive behavior is not the same as having times of relational difficulty. It is about selfishly controlling another person, which results in harm for the person involved.

We can break this down further by looking at some of the behaviors typical of an emotional abuser. Abusers commonly use verbal abuse, coercion and threats, minimizing, denying and blaming, intimidating, playing mind games, isolation, personal privilege (this term is explored later), financial control, using the children, exhibiting two different personalities, jealousy, and good periods. These behaviors work together to lead them to having control over another person.

Types of emotional abuse

Verbal abuse

If someone is being verbally abusive, they will speak in an attacking or hurtful manner, with the purpose of leading you to believe something that is not true, or they will say things to you that are not true. It involves overt and covert abuse.

Overt abuse is "openly demeaning" behavior that includes belittling, yelling, name-calling, criticizing, ordering around, sulking, accusing, ridiculing, insulting, trivializing, expressing disgust toward you, threatening, blaming, humiliating, shouting, and shaming.

Covert abuse is subtle. You are aware that something is wrong but are not certain what the real problem is. It includes discounting (when someone treats you and your opinions as unreliable or unimportant), negating (contradicting or denying things you say), accusing, denying, labeling, using subtle threats, disapproving facial expressions, a sarcastic tone of voice, implying that you are inadequate, joking to diminish you, interrupting you, and twisting and distorting what you say. For example, when they called you names, did they speak in ways that attacked your humanity or lower you to the status of an animal or a body part? At times they may have used technical language which they thought you wouldn't understand.

Coercion and threats

If the abuser uses coercion, they will try to persuade or restrain you by force. Have they threatened you? They could have made threats about things you depend on such as food, money, clothing, medicine, church life, the family, or threats about any children you have had together.

Have they threatened to withdraw emotionally, ignore you, or even to commit suicide? Have they tried to control you while trying to frighten you? Examples are leaving anonymous threats on your voicemail, removing clothing or memorabilia, slashing tires, and stealing mail. Have they used secrets that you have told them to their own advantage, or behaved in an embarrassing way in public?

I remember a church leader who would threaten his members that if they did not do what he wanted, he would tell others what they had told him in confidence.

This included confiding in him that they had been sexually abused as children.

Since you do not know whether or not they will carry out their threats, have you come to live in a state of anxiety, despair, and helplessness? If you have, the abuser could now be able to control every detail of your daily life, even to the extent of what you eat; when, where, and how you drive a car; how you dress; how you clean yourself; and what you watch on television or the internet.

Minimizing, denying, and blaming

Does your abuser habitually minimize you and attempt to invalidate your feelings and how you experience life? Minimizing includes trivializing and discounting what you think and do. They might also discount your achievements. An example would be saying, "Anyone can pass exams nowadays", if you gain a qualification that they do not have.

Do they deny that the abuse has happened or what they are clearly feeling, or the truth or reality of what you think, what you feel, your perceptions, and even claim that they know these things better than you do? Do they consistently blame you for *their* behavior? If they do, they are avoiding the things that are bothering them and the feelings that go along with them. By doing this, they are making you responsible for what they do. By blaming you, they are able to help prevent you from confronting them, and from considering their own actions.

You will be blamed because they believe that you exist to make them happy. If they are not happy, they believe that it is your fault. Using minimizing, denying, and blaming is an attempt to control your thinking so that it conforms to how they see life.

Intimidation

If they use intimidation, they may be trying to control your circumstances or to cause you to live in fear or helplessness. When they are trying to intimidate you, they might get too close to you when they are angry, block your way, claim that their behavior is an attempt to make you listen, or drive the car aggressively as a way of trying to scare you. The three most common intimidating behaviors used are threats, surveillance, and degradation (putting the person down and trying to demean them).[6] If you are living in a state of fear, you might give into their attempts to control you, even though you have not been physically hurt. If you have given in, you probably did this because you had imagined what they might do to you.

Mind games

A person who is emotionally abusing you will try to make you doubt your own thinking. If they succeed in this, it will result in you becoming dependent on them for your thinking. Various tricks are used, such as making remarks that cause confusion. Examples are, "I am telling you this for your own good", "That never happened", and "You are just imagining it."[7] The subject of conversation may be overtly or covertly changed, they may be adamant that you were thinking things that you weren't, and twist what you say. At times they may be charming toward others, causing you to doubt whether someone who is so nice could be so bad. If they accuse you of having an evil character, it could lead you to becoming confused and doubting whether you can trust your own thinking and values. This is the point when you will accept their judgments about you as being true.

"Gaslighting" is a term commonly used to explain this type of behavior. It comes from the 1938 play *Gaslight* in which a husband tries to convince his wife that she is insane so that he can steal from her. By gaslighting the abuser says and does things that leads his victim to doubt their own perceptions.

Here are some examples of what gaslighting might look like where the wife is the abuser:

- She may call you to ask you to pick something up for her, but later deny that she called.
- She may not call and ask why you did not do as she asked.

And where the husband is the abuser:

- He tells you that he likes his steak to be well-done after having told you that he always likes his steaks rare. Then, he will shout at you for the steaks being well-done because you know that he likes them rare.
- Things might be taken from you for an unknown reason, only to reappear after you

have looked for them for a long time. This could result in you thinking that you are losing your mind.

Isolation

If someone is engaging in emotional abuse, they might isolate you by removing your support system of friends and family. They will probably believe that you should be there only for their needs and that other people might help you become more independent and stronger; this is something that they do not want to happen. If they try to isolate you, they could do this by behaving in an embarrassing or rude way when you are both with others, complaining when you have contact with others, shaming or embarrassing you in front of others, accusing you of sin, stalking you, making you both move house to a remote location, or forbidding you to leave the house. Once you have become isolated, they will be able to give you false information, which then cannot be corrected by others since they are not around. This leads to you becoming mentally dependent upon them.

Personal privilege

In order for abuse to occur, there must be inequality in the relationship. If your husband is emotionally abusive, he will probably see you as his inferior regarding your gender, intelligence, and ability to use and understand logic. If a church leader is being abusive, they will use their spiritual position. If it is a parent, it will be their parental authority. If it is a wife, she will probably use the system to her advantage (we look at this in chapter five). The abuser will have some reason to think of themselves as superior to you and will relate to you as such.

Financial control

Does your abuser prevent you from paying for your expenses by failing to give you enough money? Do they deprive you of money to buy essentials while spending a lot on themselves? If you had your own bank account before you married, your spouse probably made you give it to them. If you are employed, they might make you give what you earn to them. The family assets may have been put in their name. They may have required a detailed account of everything that you spend, accompany you when you need to spend money, and require that you seek permission before you do. If they are displeased with you, they might remove your access to money, even if you have a legitimate claim to it. Since you could not survive financially without them, this will probably lead you to being under their control. A church leader might require you explain all your finances to them and gain their approval for your budget.

Using the children

If you come to the realization that you could not survive financially on your own, if your spouse is abusing you, you might continue to put up with the abuse so that you can care for your children. If your spouse senses that they are losing power over you, they might begin to verbally abuse the children. Seeing them suffer will be upsetting and distressful for you. Your spouse might demand much from them and punish them when they fail, threaten them, or say that they will harm them.

Having two personalities

Is the abuser well-liked by other people? Do outsiders think that they are an upstanding citizen? They might relate to people outside the home in a mature way. They may be calm with outsiders while being angry at home; be generous toward outsiders, but selfish at home; or promote women's rights with outsiders yet be derogatory about women when home. They may appear to be very spiritual and caring, yet in personal conversation be threatening, intimidating, and verbally abusive. Since others believe that they are an upstanding citizen, or very spiritual, you know that they will probably not believe you or think that any trouble in the relationship is your fault.

Jealousy

Is the abuser characterized by jealousy? Do they expect you to prove your love for them while being possessive of you? Do they demand that you give all your attention to them, or accuse you of being interested in other people when there is no reason to suspect this? Their jealousy, possessiveness, and suspiciousness could lead to them stalking you; for example, calling you several times a day, expecting you to spend all your free time with them, checking what you do with your time, and keeping track of your location via your cell phone's

GPS system or other device. Any achievement you make will probably be seen as competition, and as a threat to them.

> **At times they may be charming toward others, causing you to doubt whether someone who is so nice could be so bad**

Good periods

After a period of treating you badly, they might begin to treat you well. After expressing regret about their bad behavior, there could be a period when they are kind, generous, and loving. This can lead you to hope that they are changing. If you do, you will probably start to invest in the relationship again. You will probably start to trust them and become vulnerable again. In time, when they sense that they have "gotten away" with their bad behavior, it is likely that they will start to treat you badly again. This is because they believe that you belong to them and that they have regained control. These good periods are, however, part of the abusive behavior – they are not a departure from it.

3. Emotional Abuse: What it Does

What emotional abuse does

Victims often respond in certain ways. Common responses are confusion, doubt, fear, guilt, worry, inhibition, anger, shame, or a changed mental state; emotional, behavioral, and mental dependence upon the abuser; physical ailments, loneliness, depression, and sorrow. Let's take a look at each of these in turn.

Confusion

When someone emotionally abuses you, you will probably become confused. If this happens, it is easier for them to manipulate you. Do you examine all that has happened in order to find something wrong with you that caused the abuse? Do you believe that knowing this will prevent it happening in the future? Are their behaviors too confusing for you to be able to see where you are wrong? For example, they might change the subject of the conversation or be adamant that you are thinking and feeling things which you are not. They might declare their love for you, yet at the same time behave in a manner that expresses dislike for you. When they are with others, they might behave well, yet be abusive toward you behind the scenes. Do they later deny things that they have clearly said or done? If you accept what they say as true, you are inadvertently allowing them to interpret *your* experience of events. This will result in you becoming even more confused.

Doubt

They will want you to doubt yourself. They do this by trying to get you to doubt your own perceptions and thinking ability. They might say things like, "You are just angry because you are not getting your own way, so you are saying that I am mistreating you."[8] They might say that you are illogical, argumentative, selfish, and/ or always have to have your own way. They may state that your understanding of what is happening, and your feelings, are wrong. Or they could make a derogatory comment and then claim that they were only joking. If you believe them, you will come to doubt your own understanding and perceptions. This leads them to being able to control you.

Fear

Are you living in a state of fear? This comes about because you wonder what they will be like when they come home, be like at church, when the abusive behavior will start again, going over in your mind what you should have said or done during previous abusive incidents, and trying to figure out how to make them understand you.

If previous abusive incidents come to mind, you might become scared of saying or doing the wrong thing. This can lead you to being anxious when you are with them. You might watch their facial expressions, gestures, and tone of voice in order not to upset them. You could become fearful if they track your time, control who you see, and how much money you spend; how, when, and what you cook; and what you can wear. If you speak to them about their behavior and they become angry, you will probably become fearful of that anger. If they threaten you, the children, or a family pet in some way, you will almost certainly live in fear. If you give in to fear, you could end up staying at home most of the time and becoming a recluse.

Guilt

They will probably try to make you feel guilty. They could go about doing this by coercing you to do something wrong, only to say afterwards that you are a bad person for having done it. Or they might claim that not agreeing with them is unfair, or that you are oppressing them by talking to them about the way they treat you. They could (mis)quote Bible verses to you in an attempt to make you think you are disobeying God. If you agree with them that you are the guilty one, you then become responsible for the success of the relationship.

Worry

You will probably start to worry. You may worry about what they will do to you, the children, what they say and do behind your back to others, and how they will treat you when they come home. Even though it comes naturally to you to worry about how they will relate to you, this kind of thinking does not prevent or stop the abusive behavior.

Inhibition

Due to living in a state of fear of displeasing the abuser and having lost trust in your own thinking and perception, you could become inhibited – lacking in confidence. This is especially true when they engage in stalking behavior, such as calling or texting you throughout the day, checking your emails and texts, checking your location on their phone, reacting angrily or sulking when you spend time with friends or family, or criticizing your clothing. When you are with other people, you could become concerned that you don't say or do something that will trigger an angry or sulky response from the abuser. If you start responding in this way, you will become inhibited when you are with other people.

Anger

Are you angry at the way they treat you? Part of the reason for being angry could be because you are not able to change things. With time, your anger could grow into resentment. You might also be angry at yourself for giving in to their treatment, and angry at others for not doing anything about it. The anger that you experience could add to your guilt.

Shame

The shame that you experience is because you believe that you are bad. You probably think that there is something wrong with you and that you do not deserve to be accepted by others. You might feel shame because they do not love you, and for putting up with them humiliating you. The shame may lead you to become passive and helpless.

Altered mental state

Emotionally abusive behavior will affect your thinking. You might believe that you are inadequate, just as they claim. "Flooding" can occur, which is when flashbacks, intrusive thoughts, and/or painful memories bombard your thinking.[9] This will lead to your ability to think clearly and ability to judge things properly both being negatively affected. You could come to a point where you start to think that you are losing your mind. You will probably magnify their bad behavior but then minimize that bad behavior when they treat you better. Or you might magnify your faults but minimize your qualities.

If this happens, you will not be thinking biblically about yourself and may come to believe that you are inadequate in some way. You could become easily distracted and preoccupied. You might find it difficult to concentrate and have a reduced capacity to perceive, think, and reason properly. This could lead you to doubt your judgment and/or perceptions. You could become obsessive about your situation, forgetful, lose things, become accident prone, and do things as an escape, such as overeating and oversleeping.

Emotional, behavioral, and mental dependence

It is likely that you will gradually become less communicative in order to avoid upsetting them. You might even stop saying what you think altogether, because you are scared of being called names by them. You may do this at first because you want to respect them, but you will eventually come to do this more often than not because you are scared of their anger. They might demand that you do what they say in all areas of life, such as church involvement, cooking, finances, clothing, housework, and the children.[10] You will eventually try to anticipate what they are thinking and wanting. You might believe that doing this can prevent them from becoming angry or that you will eventually be loved and accepted by them. If you come to the point of thinking that your thoughts and desires are unimportant, you will probably become dependent on *their* thoughts about you and behave accordingly. You could believe that you would not be able to survive without them. If there are times when they give you the emotional connection that you crave, when they revert back to being angry you may feel devastated and try to win back their love and approval.

Physical ailments

Since the mind and the body are interconnected, your thoughts in response to the abuse may affect your physical condition. It is claimed that victims of emotional abuse characteristically suffer from headaches, respiratory problems, arthritis, bladder problems, stomach problems, sleep disturbances, weight loss or gain, back pain, palpitations, or high blood pressure.[11]

Loneliness

Trying to keep their love and acceptance, only to be confronted with recurrent abuse, leads to loneliness. This comes from a lack of relationship with the abuser and with other people who understand what's going on. Your experience might be that you have no relationships with people who actually understand you.

Depression

As well as feeling lonely in your isolated situation, you could become sad. This sadness can lead to depression. If you continue to put up with and give in to the abusive behavior, you will probably become more depressed. If you live like this for a period of time, you could end up being in a constant state of depression.

Sorrow

If you internalize the abusive treatment, you will become sorrowful. Your sorrow is over the relationship that you had hoped for but never experienced.

Mike and Amy's story

Having read extensively about emotional abuse, Mike and Amy defined it as any non-physical behavior that is designed to control, intimidate, subjugate, punish, or isolate another person, resulting in the victim becoming emotionally, behaviorally, and mentally dependent on the abuser.

They understood that the mindset of the emotional abuser is one of power, control, and entitlement. The abuser wants to have power and control over their victims, which comes from a mindset of entitlement. This mindset is expressed by common ways of behaving. If the people they treat in this way go along with this kind of behavior, there will be serious outcomes for the victim.

Being disturbed by what they had discovered, Mike and Amy wondered if the Lord would want people to accept being treated in this way, so they went back to their Bibles to discover what the Lord has to say.

4. At Odds with Your Calling

LINDA WAS TREATED in abusive ways by her husband. After a few weeks of counseling, she was instructed to examine her life to see what she was doing to cause her husband to treat her that way. Once she had done this she was told to submit and suffer for Jesus' sake.

Kevin's dad, James, shouted, screamed, mocked and insulted him. Despite being in his 20s, he was not allowed out of the house without his dad's permission. James played mind games with Kevin and told people in the church about what a difficult boy he was because he did not want to grow up. When Kevin went for help, he was told to honor his dad.

Is the well-intentioned advice these people were given correct? While submission to a husband and honoring parents are crucial and vital teaching in the Bible, is it *all* that it teaches about how we are to live when treated in abusive ways, or is there more to it?

Earlier you saw that being made in God's image involves at least three aspects. First, God exists in relationship – you too are made to relate to God and to others. Second, functionally – you represent God on earth by what you do. This includes your work and rule over creation. And third, substantively – your nature is like his. You use your powers of reasoning, possess a will, and are a moral creature.

Emotional abuse goes against each of these aspects of being made in the image of God. This means that it is totally opposed to God. It is itself sin and hinders you from living as God designed.

Relationally, it leads to being controlled by the abuser, and prevented from relating to others in loving ways. According to Scripture, this type of relating is not based on what is good for the abuser. It is based on what pleases them and keeps them happy, not on what is pleasing to the Lord. Other relationships are prevented, or damaged, so that you are controlled and live for the abuser.

Functionally, it will lead you to not working or ruling over creation for the glory of God, but doing these things to please the abuser. They might try to prevent you from developing your skills or taking a course of study to better use your God-given abilities in your daily life and workplace, or to increase your knowledge. In the church, you may be prevented from being a faithful steward of your spiritual gifts and could be hindered from developing in other areas of life, e.g. academically and musically.

Substantively, you might not be allowed to think or choose for yourself, or make decisions based on what the Lord would want. Your choices have to be about what the abuser would want. The outcome of this can be seen morally in the areas discussed in the previous chapter. For example, you might lie to someone as instructed by the abuser in order to please them and be submissive. Living in this way means you are living according to your old nature/self, not your new nature/self in Christ. It prevents you from growing and producing the fruit of the Spirit (Eph 4:20-24; Gal 5:19-21).

The importance of bringing about change

Emotional abuse is sinful and the opposite of how God commands us to treat each other as part of his creation. It is right *not* to give in to it, and it is right to *do* something about it. To live as God designed you to live means it is right to resist being treated in this way. Sometimes, well-intentioned people can (mis)quote Bible verses about being submissive to your husband or a church leader, or to honor your parents, telling you to give in to the way you are being treated. But abuse is not merely about submission and honor – it involves everything about who you are and how you live. You are being obedient to the Lord by thinking, choosing, living morally, working, and relating in ways that honor him; so it is right for you to get help so you can do this in a wise and godly way.

> **Emotional abuse is sinful and the opposite of how God commands us to treat each other as part of his creation**

Mike and Amy's story

As Mike and Amy listened to people who had been treated in emotionally abusive ways, they repeatedly heard that well-meaning people had advised them to go the extra mile, to turn the other cheek, to honor their parents, to obey their spiritual leaders, and to be submissive to their husbands. They realized that in some situations this may have been an "encyclopedic" approach to the Bible and helping people, rather than thinking in terms of the Bible as a whole.[2]

As they thought about what it means to be made in the image of God, and what the outcomes of emotional abuse are, they came to see that emotional abuse goes completely against how God designed human beings to live. Relationally, it hinders them from relating to God and others; functionally, it affects their ability to work and rule over creation; and substantively, it hinders their ability to think, reason, live morally, and make decisions that please God.

Mike and Amy were shocked to see how opposed to God's nature emotional abuse is. They saw clearly that the church should provide care and help for victims so that they can come to a place of living in the way God intends. As they sought to help equip their church to be able to provide this kind of care, Mike and Amy shared their research about what emotional abuse looks like in different relationships. Because of this, the church would become better able to recognize emotional abuse and provide the help and pastoral support needed.

---

2 An encyclopaedic approach to reading the Bible is when a person finds a Bible verse that is similar to the issue in question. It does not look at the Bible as a whole about the nature of God, people, how to change, and the issue in question.

5. Recognizing Emotional Abuse in Various Relationships

THE HUMAN HEART is the same in all people. There is no one type of person who is naturally more kind or abusive than another. Thankfully, abuse is no longer a hidden subject in society. In a lot of countries, people are encouraged to speak up and get help if they are being treated badly. This is a positive recent development which will hopefully help many as well as protect others from ever being treated in an abusive manner.

At the time that this book is being written, it is usually abuse in marriage that is discussed and that by husbands towards their wives. In this chapter, we will look at how the mindset of emotional abuse is expressed in a spectrum of relationships.

Emotional abuse in various relationships

As I've written an entire book on the subject of abusive husbands (*The Emotionally Abusive Husband*), let's begin with abusive wives. I also wanted to start here to alert the reader that emotional abuse is not a male or husband issue – it is a sin issue. Women and wives can also be guilty.

1. Wife

Although we do not hear of it often, there are wives who emotionally abuse their husbands. There are some common ways that they go about this. As well as the common emotionally abusive behaviors already described, an emotionally abusive wife may also:

- *Abuse the system.* She could try to use the legal system by threatening her husband that if he leaves her, she will make sure she gains sole custody of the children, and that he will not be able to see them. She could tell other people that the children are too scared to see him, or claim that the children have told her that he has done things to them. By claiming that he is mistreating her in some way, she could get a restraining order against him under a false pretext and may falsely claim that he has broken court orders.

- *Falsely accuse (or threaten to falsely accuse) him of domestic or sexual abuse.*

- *Isolate him from friends and relatives.* Isolation is common in abusive relationships. If a wife isolates her husband, she could go about it in various ways. She might make comments about the amount of time he spends with friends at weekends, and then put pressure on him and try to make him feel guilty by claiming that those people are more important to him than her. She could sulk or behave in inappropriate ways when they are with friends, or falsely accuse others of being interested in him romantically. If she does not want him to go out for the evening, she might try to seduce him by undressing. If he does go out, she might constantly text him, tell lies about his friends to others, tell lies about him to the friends, or even try to cause an argument between her husband and his friends. She might claim that his mother doesn't like her, that she is not good enough and never will be for his mom, and then try to manipulate situations to prove this to her husband. As well as this, she might accuse his brothers of making inappropriate comments to her or of romantically approaching her. She might persuade them to relocate far away from his side of the family.

- *Seek to control his work hours and relationships.* She will probably be upset if he works long hours and be jealous and suspicious of his female colleagues. She might try to make him work from home and prevent him from going to work social activities. If he does go to work, she could show up with the children, saying that she can't look after them on her own and that he has to come home to help.

- *Turn the children against him.* She will probably undermine him in front of the children. This is often done by going against his instructions and calling him names in front of them and/or instructing them to call him those names. She might claim that she can't cope without him and that the children may suffer because of this. In an attempt to prevent him from spending time with other people, she might use the children by claiming that it proves that his friends are more important to him than them. If she is in a new relationship, she will speak well/highly of the new partner to the children, but speak badly of him or undermine him, comparing him to the new "better" partner.

- *Harass him.* She might repeatedly phone and text him.
- *Manipulate him using technology.* If she has his passwords, she might insinuate that he is in a relationship with another woman, use his social media apps or phone messaging system to send messages to people pretending to be him, check his call logs and text messages to see who he has been talking to and what about, and/or track where he is going.
- *Use pornography.* She could make him watch pornographic material in order to make him do something that goes against his conscience and use that against him later.
- *Exercise financial control.* She could stop him from having his fair share of the household money or take his money from him. She could

prevent him from using the car or not give him enough money to be able to use public transport.

Many people believe that abuse of husbands by wives is more common than is generally thought because some men do not take the way they are being treated seriously, and so do not report the abuse. The problem of not reporting the abuse is compounded by the lack of services available to help men. Furthermore, since men are often understood as being more dominant and aggressive than women, if a man was to admit he was being abused by his wife, others might think that he is unmanly. If a husband does go along with the abuse, there are a number of areas where he will probably struggle. They include the following:

- Self-doubt. He may doubt his ability to think due to her mind games and gaslighting.
- Convinced he is going "mad" or "losing his mind".
- Anxiety, fear, and panic attacks.
- Seems afraid of, or is anxious to please his partner.
- Depression.
- Sorrow.
- A sense of helplessness.
- Stress.
- Isolation.
- Self-harm.

- Goes along with everything she says and does.
- Checks in often with his partner to report where he is and what he is doing.
- Has a very low view of himself, even if he was a confident person in the past.
- Shows major personality changes: for example, he might change from being an outgoing person to becoming withdrawn.
- Takes up or increases drink or drugs use.
- Has problems sleeping and has nightmares.
- Spends long hours in the workplace.
- Does not take his appearance seriously (being unkempt, unhygienic).
- Looks unwell (including lack of sleep/insomnia).
- Suicidal ideation and suicide attempts.[12]

2. Husband

The dynamics involved when husbands emotionally abuse their wives, and the responses of the wives, correspond with what was written previously about the behaviors and effects of emotional abuse. The personal privilege involved when husbands abuse their wives is usually related to a belief in male privilege. They believe that men are inherently superior to women because of, for example, their gender, intelligence level, and ability to use and understand logic. The husband will probably believe that proper masculinity involves a man controlling and dominating his wife and that it is unfeminine for a wife to doubt or question his instructions. He could expect his wife to allow him to make decisions while she fulfills her womanly role of cooking, cleaning, caring for the children, and catering to his every need. For more on this subject please see my other book in the series, *The Emotionally Abusive Husband*.

What if we're not married yet?

Without suggesting you become suspicious, it's important to note that emotionally abusive patterns of behavior can start to become evident before a couple get married. Addressing these may help the reader avoid or help someone else avoid a bad decision. As with Josh, whose abusive behavior is described at the start of chapter 2, things to look out for may include one or more of the following: starting to control how the other person plans to spend their money; controlling how much time they spend with others, including relatives; not being willing to admit any wrong-doing in a conflict or disagreement, but instead putting the blame solely on the other; not allowing the other person to have their own viewpoint while putting them under pressure to accept theirs as the only right perspective; and persuading the other person to come to bed. This kind of developing abusive behavior could also tip over into sexual abuse, e.g. the boyfriend persuades his girlfriend to expose herself in person or online; or rape before marriage. All this underlines the importance of pre-marital counseling as well as ensuring boyfriend and girlfriend get to know each others' families before getting serious with each other. The increase in the percentage of people beginning relationships via online dating websites makes this even more crucial. Get to know the other person's family and friends so you get a proper picture about who they are, and who and what shaped them growing up. This should naturally form part of any major relationship decision and will help you discern God's will about it.

3. Older people

What is an older person?

There is no international agreement on when someone becomes an older person, as this differs from country to country. The World Health Organization uses 60 as the age when someone would be considered an older person.[13]

What is abuse of an older person?

Abuse of an older person involves negligent behavior or willful infliction of injury, unreasonable confinement, intimidation, or cruel punishment, with resulting physical or emotional harm or pain by his or her caretaker, family member, or other individual who has an ongoing relationship with the older person. This can be a single or repeated act, or lack of appropriate action, occurring within any relationship where there is a clear expectation of trust, which causes harm or distress to the older person.[14]

What are common abusive behaviors towards older people?

There are a number of common ways that older people suffer abuse:

- Verbal abuse.
- Coercive control.
- Threatening and trying to frighten them.
- Bullying.
- Harassment.
- Mind games (gaslighting).
- Turning a blind eye.
- Ignoring them.
- Abandonment.
- Deprivation of social stimulus and pleasurable social activities.
- Isolation (from other people, relatives).

- Financial. Taking advantage of their money or property, refusing them access to their money, stealing their money, building up debt in their name, making them pay for someone else's goods, lying about the amount of money needed for their care, using their bank or credit card(s) without their permission, and tricking them into signing a contract or changing their will.

- Neglect. The carer disregards or ignores their duties toward the older person, especially those things that the older person cannot perform by themselves. Examples are eating, drinking, dressing, and the heating and lighting of the residence. It includes being left alone for very long periods of time, ignoring the older person's needs regarding medical visits, and medical tools and equipment such as hearing devices, walkers, and glasses.

- Talking to them like a child or calling them names.

- Under- or over-medicating the older person.

- Not taking them to the bathroom.

- Restricting or preventing religious or cultural practices.

- Preventing them from making their own decisions.

Outcomes of these kinds of abusive behaviors

If an older person goes along with the abusive treatment, there are a number of likely outcomes, or results, in their lives. These include:

- Anger.
- Anxiety that the person may leave them if they speak up, that they will be left without support, or that they will lose relationships with other family members such as their grandchildren.
- Worry that they won't be believed.
- Shyness.
- Uneasiness.
- Weak eye contact.
- Depression.
- Self-blame.
- Guilt.
- Hopelessness if they have already received a negative response from agencies when they first reported the abuse.
- Excessive crying.
- Suicidal ideation.
- Talk badly about themselves.
- Hesitant to speak openly.
- Upset or agitated.
- Withdrawn and uncommunicative or non-responsive.
- Confused.
- Disoriented.

- Restless.
- Suspicious.
- Sudden change of, or unusual behavior, e.g. sucking, biting, or rocking.
- Hoarding.
- Changes in sleeping patterns.
- Weight changes.
- Bad hygiene.
- Unkempt (inadequately clothed).
- Living in a chaotic or dilapidated environment.
- Insufficient food (malnourished or dehydrated, lack of assistance in eating and drinking).
- Lacking eye glasses, dental false teeth, walkers, and/or wheelchair.
- Dirt, fecal or urine smell, or other health and safety hazards in their living environment.
- Rashes, sores, or lice.
- Untreated medical condition.[15]

The importance of community

This is covered in chapter 10, but just to note here that it is crucial that local churches supporting older people work with any social care / services or other facilities available locally. It is important for people to visit the older person regularly. This ensures that they can keep track of how the older person is and view their living conditions. By visiting on a regular basis, it will be more difficult for the abuser to isolate them.

In some places, such as the United Kingdom, if there are concerns about how an older person is being treated by their carer, they will be offered some form of respite care on an inpatient or day-care basis. Formal services can be increased and the situation monitored. If a crime has been committed, this should be reported to the local police. Laws differ, so please inform yourself about what the laws in your area are regarding the care of older people. This will of course vary depending on the country or state you live in.

When you visit an older person, let them know that you care, want to listen, and are willing to do what you can to help. If the older person reveals to you what is going on, it could be quite distressing for them. Please be aware of this and show sensitive support as you lovingly listen.

4. Parent

There are a number of ways that emotionally abusive parents treat their children. These include the following:

- Calling the child derogatory names, ridiculing, scolding, blaming, humiliating, verbally attacking, or belittling the child.
- Displaying an ongoing pattern of negativity or hostility toward the child; examples are refusing to talk to the child, giving hateful looks, and undermining the child for who they are, their gender, and what they do.

- Making excessive and/or inappropriate demands of the child.
- Exposing the child to extreme or unpredictable caregiver behaviors.
- Using fear, intimidation, humiliation, threats, or bullying to discipline the child, or pressuring the child to keep secrets. The parent may threaten abandonment and/or expose the child to situations that are scary and overwhelming.
- Demonstrating a pattern of boundary violations, excessive monitoring, or overcontrol that is inappropriate considering the child's age.
- Expecting the child to assume an inappropriate level of responsibility or placing them in role reversal, such as frequently taking care of younger siblings or attending to the emotional needs of the caregiver.
- Undermining the child's significant relationships.
- Not allowing the child to engage in age-appropriate socialization.

If you had emotionally abusive parents, they will have been manipulative, and could have kept information from you, accused you of being or doing what the parent was being or doing, and talked to others about you instead of talking to you directly. They may have put you down, refused to take responsibility, refused to speak to you for periods of time, and ignored you. They may have twisted what you thought and felt, humiliated you in front of others by making fun of you, slandered you to others, undermined you, minimized what you thought and did, and mocked you. When they portrayed themselves as a good person to others, they communicated concern about their 'troubled child', giving the impression that you were problematic.

Four layers to the behavior of emotionally abusive mothers have been observed. These are:

1. *Admiration*. This is their attitude to life. They want and expect to be admired, listened to, and agreed with.

2. *Fear*. If people do not admire them, they will try to make them afraid. At this point they will enter into what is known as "narcissistic rage".[3]

3. *Pity*. If fear does not work, they will try to gain other people's pity by playing the victim.

4. *Vindictive*. If pity does not work, they will become vindictive and start a smear campaign.[16]

Many abusive parents engage in what are known as the three D's: drama, denial, and deflection.

1. **Drama:** If they are challenged or criticized, they will react in a dramatic way.

2. **Denial:** If drama does not work, they will deny that they had said or did what they are being challenged about. The parent will say that you

---

3 The Bible does not use the word "narcissist," but it does address the motives and behaviors that are involved. According to the Bible, narcissism is insolent pride. For more information see https://biblicalperspectivesonnarcissism.com/2018/12/06/narcissism-insolent-pride-in-the-bible/

did not see what you saw, that you are imagining things, or that you are dreaming.

3. **Deflection:** If denial does not work, they will engage in deflection. For example, if they are faced with criticism, or are challenged, they will change the topic onto the person who is criticizing them. In the process, the discussion becomes about the other person's faults and shortcomings instead of the issue that was raised. By doing this, they do not have to admit that they have done or said anything wrong.

If these do not work, they might say that they are sorry, but do so in a way that puts the blame on you. Examples are, "I am sorry you can't take a joke", or, "I am sorry that you got upset". If they apologize in this way, they expect that life will go on as if nothing has happened. However, if they think that *you* have done something wrong, they make you apologize until they find the level of the apology acceptable enough.1718

The effects of emotionally abusive parents and how to overcome them in Christ have been dealt with extensively in the book, *The Emotionally Abusive Parent.*

5. Siblings

What is sibling abuse?

It is difficult to know the difference between normal sibling conflict and what would be considered emotionally abusive behavior. It has been suggested that it can be known by its constancy (how often the behavior occurs) and intensity (how severe the behavior is).

When we think of siblings, we are not only talking about biological siblings from both parents. They can be biological (the same biological parents), step-siblings (through their parents marrying), half-siblings (when they share one biological parent), or they could be siblings through foster care or adoption. In all cases, when the abuse occurred, they were part of the same family unit.

What does sibling abuse involve?

- Lying regularly (especially when it could lead to other people thinking badly about their sibling and therefore ruining their reputation).
- Name calling.
- Ridiculing.
- Degrading (putting their sibling down and trying to demean them).
- Belittling.
- Intimidating.
- Threatening violence.
- Harassment.
- Humiliating.
- Scorning.
- Gossiping.
- Encouraging others to isolate their sibling.
- Provoking.

- Putting them down in relation to their opinions and the things they are seeking to accomplish.
- Saying that they will fail at everything they attempt.
- Blaming their sibling when things do not go well, even if he/she had no direct control over the situation.
- Make derogatory and insulting comments about their appearance.
- Responding with hostility and defensiveness if they speak to them about their problems and then they find ways to take revenge.
- Making fun of their sibling, for example the hobbies or friends they have.
- Chameleon-like behavior by changing their behavior according to the person that they are with.
- Destroying their sibling's personal possessions.
- Harming or killing the sibling's pets.
- Cyber-bullying.
- Excluding them from a group they would naturally expect to be part of.
- Group teasing (the habit of urging their group of friends to tease their sibling).

Common outcomes of sibling abuse

- Crying, screaming, or hiding in an attempt to isolate themself from the abuser.

- Thinking suicidal thoughts.
- Holding a low view of who they are in comparison to other people.
- Being dependent on the abuser.
- Physiological complaints.
- Depression.
- Nightmares.
- Aggressiveness.
- Fear and anxiety.
- Phobias.
- Apathy.
- Confusion.
- Over- or under-achievement in education.

It is quite common for parents to fail to take their child seriously when they tell them about the abusive behavior. Usually, parents respond by saying that it is normal sibling rivalry. Parents might believe the victim is being difficult or is responding in the way they do because of a disability they have.

It is important for parents to examine how they relate to each child and what the dynamics are in the home. If they have treated one child as superior, the victim might believe that they are inferior. It is important for parents to examine how they treat each member of the family, address problem areas, and seek to relate to everyone in God-honoring ways.[19]

6. People with disabilities

Somebody who has a disability has a physical or mental impairment that, in the long-term, limits their ability to carry out daily activities.[4] The person with the disability will probably need help from other people, or carers, to carry out these tasks. Sometimes carers can be abusive by engaging in coercive and controlling behavior toward them.

Common types of emotionally abusive behaviors toward people with disabilities include:

- Name calling.
- Guilt-tripping (the carer or family member ensures that the person with the disability feels guilty about the care they are receiving and the activities the carer / family member may have missed out on as a result).
- Withholding medication, or over-medicating.
- Destroying or disabling equipment.
- Withholding assistance in preparing food and drink.
- Giving them food which is too hot.
- Financial abuse.

People who have disabilities suffer similar effects as other victims of emotional abuse which we have explored in this chapter. Many people with disabilities who are experiencing abuse are too afraid to speak up because

4 Equality Act 2010: https://www.legislation.gov.uk/ukpga/2010/15/section/6 (Accessed June 25, 2022).

they are dependent on the abuser and fear what might happen to them since they cannot look after themselves. It is also common for victims to think that no one will believe them. They may fear that reporting the abuse will mean that they won't be able to live at home anymore and will have to move to a care facility. Since they are dependent on a carer, who could be the person who is abusive toward them, it is advisable that anyone from the church wanting to provide help or intervention seeks advice from local groups who can inform them about what legal issues are involved and how to protect the person with the disability from current or possible future abuse.[20]

6. Recognizing Emotional Abuse in Church and Other Ministry Contexts

1. Spiritual leaders

SADLY, PEOPLE IN various positions of leadership in churches, Christian organizations and parachurch ministries can emotionally abuse those under their care. This is also described as spiritual abuse. Great care must be taken in this area. At times, the nature of the local church and various leaders within it, as well as leadership roles in Christian organizations, involves speaking to people about their lives, instructing and correcting them, and, in the case of the local church, possibly implementing church discipline. Church discipline is when someone is removed from the church as part of the process of trying to help them deal with sin in their lives and to be restored to relationship with God and others (Matthew 18:15-20; 1 Corinthians 5). Church leaders should be willing to do these things; done correctly it is not abuse. In the case of ministry organizations, where many people involved are employed, there will be employment and other laws to consider, but these are beyond the scope of this book.

Spiritual abuse is coercion and control of one individual by another in a spiritual context. The abuse may include:

- Manipulation and exploitation.
- Enforced accountability.
- Bullying.
- Belittling.
- Threatening.
- Threats of being punished by God if they do not obey the leader.
- Censorship of decision making.
- Requirements for secrecy and silence.
- Pressure to conform.
- Misuse of Scripture or the pulpit to control behaviour in an attempt to get them to do what the leader wants.
- Requirement of obedience to the abuser, suggesting that they hold a "divine" position.
- Isolation from others (especially those external to the abusive context such as family or friends).
- Financial control. Consistent and excessive pressure to give specific amounts or percentages of income, and/or for individuals to make huge sacrifices for the church or organization, while the leaders use the money for their own purposes.

Common signs of spiritual abuse among leaders

These are not exhaustive but simply to alert you to the kinds of behaviors consistent with abusive leader(s). Some of them overlap. It is also important to note that if some of these occur, it does not mean the leader is an emotional abuser, rather that they have committed an emotionally / spiritually abusive act. For example, leader A might make one or two poor decisions and misuse their power, which is correctly seen as being abusive. But he / she sincerely repents when challenged, whatever the consequences; there is no evidence of historic patterns of abuse. But in another church or organization it comes out in an investigation that leader B has been exhibiting many of the signs of abusive behavior for years. Many people simply did not realize; others chose to turn a blind eye or accommodate the behavior since leader B was so influential. Leader A does not have an emotionally abusive mindset; leader B does, and will hopefully come to realize this.

The more of the following you can see in your context, the more likely some sort of emotional / spiritual abuse is going on.

Leader responses

- The leader gets angry or into a rage if someone says something that is understood to be unacceptable. This may be done behind the scenes; most people don't know about it, but those at the receiving end certainly do.

- Double talk. The leader will seldom say what they mean. Things are veiled, or hidden, or else people are told they are not spiritual enough to understand the teachings or decisions of the leaders.
- The leader is defensive and portrays themselves as a victim if they are under attack.
- Leader exhibits impatience or a lack of ability to listen to others.
- Leader feels entitled.
- Feeling threatened or intimidated by other talented staff.
- Needing to be the best or the brightest in the room.
- Leader only admits doing wrong in order to get out of a difficult situation – it is not sincere. This is known as 'fauxpology'.[5]
- The leader's home life is portrayed as perfect or is not accessible.

Power, position and image

- The leader's focus is on themselves and not the needs of the flock (see Ezekiel 34).
- The leader has a group of close followers around them who are in the know and who protect them from criticism and support their power and position.

---

5 A fauxpology is a false apology that you say or write in order to tell someone that you are sorry (but don't really mean it).

- The leader wants approval and adoration, rejects criticism, and uses their position to serve themselves. The leader's actions are seen to be more important than the needs of church members, even if it causes them harm.

- The leader uses their position, verbal power, and theological knowledge to get people to do what they want and to praise them.

- Words like 'obedience' and 'submission' are often used.

- The lives of church members or those committed to the ministry or organization are controlled by rules.

- Problematic situations are protected by silence or assault. If someone speaks about the issues, *they* become the problem.

- The place of honor. Things are done so that the leader is well spoken of and honored. If the leader does not receive the place of honor they desire, they will make sure that no one else does either.

- Image is everything. The leader keeps up a (false) image. What matters is how things look. The leader demands performance from the church members to ensure that the leaders and/ or the church's image is consistently portrayed to others.

- Structure. The church functions in a way that it props up those in leadership, while ensuring that other people are kept submissive. This can be done on the basis of their sex, social status, how much theology they understand, and how gifted they are.

- Loyalty to the leader is demanded.
- The ministry is portrayed as being specially blessed by God and to question it is to question what God is blessing, e.g. "Touch not the Lord's anointed" (Psalm 105:15).

How people are treated / tend to respond

- The leader cuts someone off from contact with the group. For example, a person may be removed over time by someone who holds a lot of influence over a particular area of church life, and/or the leader(s) make others doubt their integrity and block them from ministry.
- People are removed from the group if they disagree with the leader.
- Those in the group are instructed not to speak with the person who has been removed.
- Spirituality is used to make others live up to certain standards. Being in a right standing with God includes additional spiritual acts of service the leader insists on.
- Church members are given the impression that they are less than spiritual if they have problems with what the leader says or wants or won't comply.
- Church members are shamed. Examples include correcting them in public when unnecessary,

or requiring other members to shun them after they are thrown out; those who are understood to be less spiritual, well connected, charismatic, intelligent, or powerful are also shamed.

- Those who obey the leader are rewarded, whereas those who do not are ignored and others are told to ignore them.

- People are expected to sacrifice much in the name of God.

- Other churches are portrayed as being less spiritual, blessed, faithful, or biblical.

- Using the provision of previous, sometimes substantial, support for an individual/congregant (be it financial, emotional, practical, etc.) as justification for control, harshness, demands for loyalty or other things, and support for the leaders.

- People are very careful or afraid of what they say to the leader.

- Some, even those who are part of the leader's inner circle, can be end up being deceived as to the reality of the abuse taking place, preferring instead to uphold the leader and disbelieving anyone who makes an allegation of abuse. Others may not be deceived but still afraid.

- Only after an impartial investigation, perhaps by an outside agency brought in after a build-up of complaints of abuse, will some people (including those close to the leader) fully realize the true nature and extent of the abuse that had been occurring.

The Bible and/or prophecy

- The leader is focused on their authority and reminds others of it by citing certain Scriptures, the importance of leaders or leadership, or the centrality of seeing the vision go forward.
- People cannot know or understand truths until the leaders receive them by spiritual revelation from the Lord and impart them to the people.
- The Bible is used to help the leader get what they want – this is called "proof-texting" when someone has a point they want to prove.
- Church members are treated as if they have little or no capacity to discern God's Word for themselves and therefore depend on the leader to understand it.

Accountability

- The leader is not corrected if they say something that is clearly unbiblical or abusive.
- The leader is not held accountable via any formal processes (e.g. how they use funds) and does not accept criticism, e.g. no feedback loop to hear any concerns or comments.
- All decision-making centers on the leader.

- Delegation without giving proper authority or with too many limits.
- Control. Anything that does not support the system and its effective functioning is controlled.

Abusive leaders who avoid conflict

- Making others do unpopular tasks, such as correcting people, so that the leader is always seen as a nice person.
- Hiding behind the inability to speak the truth to others, and speaking "variations of the truth" to appease whoever they are with at the time.
- Being unwilling/unable to correct their own family members when necessary. A leader's family can often have a powerful impact on the life of the church.
- Lack of ownership regarding poor decisions.
- Refusal to gather all parties together to resolve conflict. This keeps the leader in 'good graces' because he doesn't have to correct anyone.

2. The church or ministry as a system needing protected

When people have the courage to speak up about an abusive system, they are often met with resistance because they are understood to be attacking God's church or a particular ministry. The church or ministry ends up being protected rather than the issues involved investigated and dealt with properly. In the process, victims and those who speak up are often portrayed as liars, divisive, negative, and insubordinate.

Outcomes

A spiritually abusive system works because the people who remain part of it tend to be people who want to be in the inner circle and desire approval and affirmation. The impact on the group is divided into those who follow the leader and those who are perceived as being disobedient. Those who remain part of the group become loyal to the leader. Questioning, or criticizing them, is seen as questioning God, or the questioner is understood to be sinning by doing so.

If someone believes what a supposed man (or woman) of God says about them, they could come to believe that they are without value, less than other people, that other people do not care, and even that God does not care about them. Due to the way they were treated when they spoke up, it is likely that they will struggle to trust people again. They will probably be judged, condemned, confused, shamed, and carry a lot of guilt as a person and as a Christian. Since they thought the leader was a spiritual person, but turned out to be an abuser, they will probably be confused. They could be afraid of saying anything because of the harm it could cause them if the leader was to speak against them, or the damage it could do to the church / ministry. Many will blame themselves, thinking that if they had not said or done certain things, everything would be different.

The most common outcomes

- A distorted image of God. They could come to understand God as never satisfied, mean and vindictive – that he watches and waits for us to make mistakes and doesn't care or help when people are hurt or abused.
- A preoccupation with spiritual performance. This usually leads to self-righteousness or shame.
- An unbiblical view of self, based on shame and failure.
- Problems relating to those with spiritual authority. They could develop ways of defending themselves from further abuse, either being compliant or defiant toward authority.
- Misunderstanding grace due to the works-based philosophy of the group.
- Problems setting limits. This has come about because the spiritual leader has misused their power to cross limits, or boundaries, by accusing the church member of being selfish, sinning, or being unspiritual if they did not do what they wanted.
- Could struggle with personal responsibility. If that's you, you might fail to take responsibility before God for other people you should care

for, because you know that no matter what you do, it is never enough to bring you love and acceptance. Or, you could become over-responsible – living as if you are responsible for solving everybody's issues.

- You may suffer from a lack of living skills due to being closed off from the outside world and keeping things that go on in the group a secret.
- You may find it difficult to admit the abuse. Abusive leaders accuse those who notice the problem of being the problem, making it difficult to expose what has gone on, even after you have left the church. For many, admitting that the church is abusive feels like they are being disloyal to the church and maybe even to God.
- Learned powerlessness. Those in an abusive system will not be taught the skills needed to make biblical life choices. Someone in this position may even believe that they are less able to make decisions or are weaker than other people, simply because of who they are.

3. Reasons why people stay in abusive systems

What causes people to stay in a church or ministry where there is spiritual abuse? There are a number of possible reasons:

- They do not want to lose their friends, or family, and the years they have invested in the church.

- Fear of the abuser carrying out any threats that he has made to harm them, their friends, or their family.
- Fear of being humiliated or slandered in front of others, or their secrets being told to others.
- Dependence on the abuser and not knowing if they could survive emotionally or financially without them.
- Since they believe that the abuse is their fault, they could believe that they deserve the way that they have been treated.
- Things improve for a short time when they are about to leave, which leads to them changing their minds.
- They believe what the abuser has told them about themselves, other people, or God, even though these things are not true
- They do not want the reputation of the church, and therefore God's reputation, harmed by leaving, or raising issues.
- They believe that people outside of the church do not understand the church.
- They believe that they will in some sense be unsafe if they leave the church.
- They believe that being disloyal to the leader is sinful and, to some extent, being disloyal to God.
- They could believe that if they leave, God will withdraw his blessing and they and their family will be at risk of spiritual attack as a result.

4. Common ways Scriptures are misused by those with an abusive mindset

There are some Bible verses which are commonly wrongly used in order to manipulate people into doing what the abuser wants. Here are some examples:

- *The concept of self-denial* (Matthew 16:24). Self-denial is often used as a way of trying to get church members to do what the leadership wants.

- *Giving* (Deuteronomy 14:22-23; Malachi 3:8; 2 Corinthians 9:6 and 16:1-2). People are pressured into giving in order to be accepted by the group and to stay in God's favor. This includes forcing the issue of the tithe, an Old Testament concept but a good principle. There are differences of opinion about whether or not, and to what extent, this concept is applicable in the life of a Christian.

- *Unity and peace in the church* (Matthew 5:9; Philippians 2:2; Ephesians 4:3). People are pressured into thinking and behaving the way that the leader wants, while they claim that it is part of being united, and that any other views are divisive.

- *Church discipline* (Matthew 18;15-17; 1 Corinthians 5:5). People are threatened with some form of church discipline if they do not do what the leader wants, or church discipline is used against them if they are not obedient to them.

- *Never resist* (Matthew 5:39). Church members are sometimes taught that they should not resist or oppose anything sinful or harmful.

- *Just forgive* (Matthew 18:21-22). Church members are taught that they always have to forgive and move on. They are taught that if they forgive as they should, the offender should experience no repercussions or consequences for what they have done.

- *Never appeal to secular authorities* (1 Corinthians 6:1-7). It is taught that it is sinful to report things to people outside the church. Church members are discouraged from reporting alleged criminal behavior to the police or to any legal authority. However, 1 Corinthians 6:1-7 is not addressing an allegation of criminal behavior but a civil dispute, likely involving money or property since Paul then writes about someone being 'defrauded'. But if criminal behavior *is* suspected, Christians should be submissive to the governing bodies by reporting it according their government's laws, as taught in Romans 13:1-7.

- *Never deal with the past* (Philippians 3:13-14). If church members still struggle with things from their past, such as abuse, they could have been told that they have to forget about it and move on. However, this passage is talking about reliance on spiritual performance to obtain a good standing with God, not about getting help for things that are still troublesome.

- *Unquestioned authority* (Hebrews 13:17; 1 Thessalonians 5:12-13). Church members are taught that they have to obey the leaders in everything they ask.21

5. The nature of true spiritual authority

Abusive leaders enforce people to live according to their rules. This is contrary to the gospel and what Jesus has done and wants to do in our lives.

Spiritual authority is delegated. It is given so that the leaders lovingly care for the church members in order to help them lead Christlike lives. They are to shepherd the flock as under-shepherds of the Chief Shepherd – the Lord Jesus. Instead of being domineering, they are to be examples to church members.

Real authority is found in the Lord and his Word, not in the church leader or leaders as a person or people. The leader(s) should be placing themselves under that authority and not make it about them. Church members are to be encouraged to be loyal and obey Jesus, not simply to church leader(s).

There should be confidential channels for raising concerns, and these should be well publicized. Those who speak up about abuse should be protected, not punished. A suggestion is to consider the development of a safeguarding procedure. If a safeguarding procedure is set up, it needs to be done well, according to the type of church, denomination, or organization involved. There have been many times when people who did speak up were not protected by the church authorities, which resulted in them being punished in some way.[6]

Mike and Amy's story

Mike and Amy shared their findings about emotional abuse with other people in the church. In their research they tried to cover as many relationships and situations that they could, including wife to husband, husband to wife, spiritual leaders, older people, parents, siblings, and people with disabilities. Although it was disturbing to read this material, they felt better able to recognize signs of abuse. Mike and Amy then moved on to learn what the Bible teaches about how the church can provide help and care.

6 In the United Kingdom, thirtyone:eight is an independent Christian safeguarding charity which helps individuals, organizations, charities, faith and community groups to protect vulnerable people from abuse. If you are interested in how they could be of assistance, please take a look at their website: https://thirtyoneeight.org/.

Section II

7. Living in the renewed image of God

HAVING EXAMINED WHAT the mindset of an emotional abuser is, how this is expressed across a spectrum of relationships in life, and the typical outcomes are for victims, this short chapter summarizes some important New Testament verses about our renewed image in Christ and our responsibility in situations of emotional abuse. Chapter 8 explores how we can begin to address the specific effects of emotional abuse.

Paul goes to great lengths to teach that all believers are called to live for righteousness (Romans 6:12-14). Regardless of a believer's circumstances, their purpose in life is to live for the glory of God (Isaiah 43:7). That is our calling and purpose. We have been saved from alienation and hostility in our minds in order to be holy and blameless before God (Colossians 1:21-22); we were chosen to be holy and blameless before him (Ephesians 1:4); we are to be conformed to the image of God's Son (Romans 8:29); and we are called to obey the Lord (1 Peter 1:2).

The renewed image in Christ

We are renewed in Jesus and called to live for his glory. Who we really are, is who he has made us. This includes being:

- Blessed in Christ with every spiritual blessing in the heavenly places (Ephesians 1:3).
- Chosen before the foundation of the world to be holy and blameless (Ephesians 1:4).
- Predestined for adoption (Ephesians 1:5).
- Redeemed through his blood and forgiven of sin (Ephesians 1:7).
- The recipient of an inheritance (Ephesians 1:11).
- Predestined to be to the praise of his glory (Ephesians 1:11).
- Sealed with the Holy Spirit as a guarantee of our inheritance (Ephesians 1:13-14).
- Complete in Christ (Colossians 2:10).

You are responsible and accountable to God for your thoughts and behavior. This is something that you should never give to another person by allowing them to control you, or your thinking. In an emotionally abusive relationship, the abuser uses things such as fear, guilt, shame, insinuations, and accusations in order to control you. If you go along with this, you will end up living in fear, guilt, shame, and believing falsehoods about yourself. These heart issues belong to the old nature, from which the Lord Jesus has redeemed you to live a new life. It is contrary to your calling to accept emotionally abusive behavior.

What will probably surprise you as you read this, is that if you accept abusive behaviors such as anger, (veiled) threats, jealousy, and punishments, you are inadvertently enabling the abuser to live according to their old nature. As believers, we are to help others become like Jesus. You are actually obeying the Lord if you seek godly help from others. It is important that you appreciate that you are *not responsible* for ensuring that the abuser is happy and not angry or jealous. They are responsible before God, and will have to give an account to him for their own mindset, emotions, and behavior.

> **It is contrary to your calling to accept emotionally abusive behavior**

Mike and Amy's story

As they started out looking at what the Bible teaches about how Christians should live, Mike and Amy saw that who a believer is depends on who Jesus is and what he has done for them, and that they are called to live according to who Jesus says they are. It was clear to Mike and Amy that these things look very different where emotionally abusive behavior and its various outcomes are concerned. They also saw that the victim is not responsible for the abuser's mindset or emotions, only for their <u>own</u> mindset and emotions and how they relate to them. It was quite an eye-opener for them to then realize that a believer is obeying the Lord by refusing to go along with abuse, and by getting help for all involved to live to honor God.

8. Effective and Lasting Change

Pastor Brian started to wonder how best to help the people who came to his church for advice. Recently, Chris had shared with Brian about his ongoing struggle with anger about the way that his dad had treated him. Pastor Brian listened attentively and after 10 minutes advised Chris that he had to let go of the things that he was angry about and trust God. Chris knew the pastor meant well, but even after praying and giving everything over to God, he still battled with anger regularly.

Then there was old Margaret. She came asking for help as she was worried about who would look after her if she did anything about the way her carer was treating her. Being 82, and on her own, Margaret's biggest fear was that she would have to enter a care facility as she could not look after herself. Pastor Brian told her that it was sinful to worry and she was to think about what is true instead. Margaret continued to be filled with worrisome thoughts. "Easier said than done," was her reply.

Joe pleaded with Pastor Brian for advice about how to relate to his abusive wife. Pastor Brian told him to be a man. Yet when Joe asked him how to be a man, he could not answer him. After years of similar stories, Pastor Brian came to realize that while his advice was well-intentioned, he wasn't helping people. Actually, he was making them feel guilty because his supposedly biblical advice did not help bring about change. Pastor Brian was humble enough to see that given the number of people involved, there was something lacking in his own understanding about how the Holy Spirit changes people from within.

Changing from within

The Bible uses different Greek words inter-changeably to describe the inner person. These include:

- Heart *(kardia* – Matthew 19:8).
- Mind *(dianonia* – Matthew 22:37; *phrenes* – Romans 8:6; *nous* – Luke 24:45).
- Soul *(psuche* – Matthew 11:29).
- Conscience *(suneidesis* – 2 Corinthians 1:12).
- Inner self *(kruptos* – 1 Peter 3:4).
- Inner man *(eso* – 2 Corinthians 4:16).[22]

These terms can be summarized by the word "heart", referring to the core of a person; that is, to his or her character. It is the non-physical part of what it means to be human.[23] The heart of a person is where his or her thoughts, will, speech, and attitudes originate.[24] It is our moral center and where we decide whether we will live for God, who we will worship, and who we will love.[25]

What heart change is

Whatever is going on in your heart will determine how you function. Jesus teaches in Mark 7:21-23 that whatever comes out of your heart defiles you. It is what you are thinking in your heart that determines your response to the abuse.

Are you like a lot of abuse victims, for whom peace is one of the most important priorities in their lives, even if it means tolerating evil on the part of the abuser? You may crave to be loved and accepted so much that you will endure the abusive behavior, hoping that by doing so you will win the abuser's love; or you might believe that you can no longer handle your situation and give up. You will probably have built patterns of thinking and behavior based on what you have thought in your heart when you were treated in an abusive way.

Living according to your purpose involves having the mind of Christ. Up until now, you might have accepted what your abuser has told you. Learning to think in ways that honor the Lord will involve testing any accusations, insinuations, exaggerations, twisting of facts, and/or use of guilt by what the Bible teaches about who Jesus is, what he says about you, and what he says about how you should live. After testing these things, it is very important that you believe and apply biblical teaching on these matters in your life.

Scriptural answers

There are a number of heart issues that you might struggle with. Jesus has answers for each of these issues in Scripture!

Confusion and doubt

Understanding that you are to have the mind of Christ will help you come out of the state of confusion and doubt that you have been in. Instead of blindly believing whatever accusations your abuser makes about how bad you are, you can live in and through Jesus. This will help you better discern when they try to shift blame onto you. If they deny having done or said something which they *did* say or do, it will help you not to accept the denial as being the truth.

Someone who switches from being loving and charming to being angry and cruel can eventually lose their hold over you. Your motive will no longer be to try to ensure that they start treating you kindly or try to stop their cruel behavior, because your motive is to live and relate to them in a way that honors Jesus. In time, it is possible that you will no longer be susceptible to their mind-games, will stop second-guessing how they will respond to you, will no longer doubt your own ability to perceive life, and will no longer continue to blame yourself for everything. As a result, your abuser will no longer be able to control your thinking.

Worry

Worry involves being preoccupied with or "overly concerned" about something.26 The main New Testament passages that address the issue of worry are Matthew 6:19-34 and Philippians 4:4-9.

Biblical instruction for dealing with worry

Matthew 6:19-34 instructs us not lay up treasure on earth; we are to lay up treasure in heaven where it cannot be destroyed. You and I can discover what our treasure is by finding out what it is that we worry about. You might be tempted to worry about how to ensure that your abuser is not angry with you, other people, or things in life that do not work out as they desire. You might worry about how to gain their love and acceptance, how you could survive (both mentally and financially) if they left you, and about your children suffering if they chose to punish them because they are angry with you (or them) for some reason.

This passage teaches that you are not to worry because God cares for his creation. Since you are much more valuable than the birds and flowers of creation that God cares for, you can be certain that he will take care of you. Thankfully, he also shows you what to focus on instead of worrying. You are called to seek God's kingdom first. This means putting God's reign, his rule first your life, praying for his kingdom to come and his reign to impact those you come into contact with, or who God has laid on our heart to pray for.

Philippians 4:4-9 instructs believers to rejoice in the Lord, not to be anxious but to be prayerful, and to think in ways that honor God. To help you rejoice in the Lord you could make a list of God's attributes and think about how a particular aspect of who God is relates to whatever you are worrying about. You could also write down what God has done in your life up until the present day. Seeing the way in which he has cared for you and worked in your life in the past will help reassure you that the Lord will keep his promises in relation to your concerns about the present and the future.

It is possible to learn to pray about these issues in a thankful way. Your thankfulness is toward the Lord because you know that he will care for you. When you do this, God promises that his peace will guard your mind and heart. Peter gives similar teaching. He instructs believers: "Humble yourselves, therefore, under the mighty hand of God so that at the proper time he may exalt you, casting all your anxieties on him, because he cares for you" (1 Peter 5:6-7).

To help you to ponder what is true, honorable, just, pure, lovely, commendable, excellent, and praise-worthy (Philippians 4:8), you could make a list of the thoughts that you have when you worry, and ask yourself if these thoughts correspond with the kinds of thoughts described in this verse. It is helpful to then think about how God's attributes and promises are true regarding those specific issues that you tend to worry about.

Fear

You could be fearful of what your abuser might do to you, afraid of speaking about them in a negative way to others. You might be afraid of speaking to your church leaders about the way they are treating you. You may believe that you would be disloyal to the abuser if you tell others.

The fear that you experience may be the result of direct or veiled threats that they have made toward you, or what you imagine might happen to you if you were to upset them too much. Anyone who lives in fear becomes paralyzed from taking action. If you are dependent on them both mentally and financially, you could fear being rejected or abandoned by them because you think you would not be able to survive without them.

Fear of man

The fear of man is, "Any anxiety that is caused by real or imagined discomfort, rejection, or danger being imposed on another human being."27 It involves trying to ensure that we do not upset people more than being concerned about honoring God. It is an "Inordinate desire for people's approval", or an "Inordinate fear of their rejection."28 People who fear others will study their body language, likes and dislikes. They are unlikely to question the views of others and will react to conflict by giving in, withdrawing, or steering the conversation onto another topic.

Fear of God

If you are afraid of people, you will probably struggle to fear God. Knowing who God is conquers the fear of man. Understanding his providence over believers is important. God's providence is as follows:

> *"God is continually involved with all created things in such a way that he (1) keeps them existing and maintaining the properties with which he created them; (2) cooperates with created things in every action, directing their distinctive properties to cause them to act as they do; and (3) directs them to fulfil his purposes."*[29]

> *"God is directing all things to fulfil his purposes. He is in control and working according to his plan in your life. Fearing God includes the knowledge that you are by nature unclean and deserve to be punished by a holy God. It also includes the knowledge that because you have trusted Jesus you have been made righteous by him. Understanding the work of Jesus on the cross will lead you to worship and trust him."*[30]

Trusting the God of Scripture

In the Bible, we discover that fear originated in Genesis 3:7-8 when Adam and Eve hid from God after they disobeyed his command not to eat from the tree of the knowledge of good and evil. Later, the people of Israel gave in to fear when they saw the giants in the land of Canaan; they did not trust that God could lead them into the promised land and help them defeat their enemies (Numbers 13:25-33). In Deuteronomy, God tells Moses not to be afraid of Og King of Bashan because he had already given Og into Moses' hand (Deuteronomy 3:2). Moses instructed Joshua not to fear the other nations because the Lord would fight for him, and told the people of Israel not to be afraid of the nations (Deuteronomy 3:22). Instead of being afraid, they were to remember what the Lord did to Pharaoh (Deuteronomy 7:17-18). Joshua was commanded not to be afraid of the nations because the Lord was with him (Joshua 1:9). He then instructed the chiefs of the men of war not to be afraid but to be courageous, because the Lord would help them against their enemies (Joshua 10:25).

David wrote about fear in many of his Psalms. For example, in Psalm 23:4 he wrote that he feared no evil because the Lord was with him: God's rod and staff brought David comfort. In Psalm 27:1-2 we read that David refused to be afraid of his enemies because the Lord was his light, salvation and stronghold. In Psalm 3, although David knew that his enemies surrounded him, he trusted the Lord as his protector.

In Jeremiah 17:5-8, we read that the person who puts their trust in people and turns away from God will suffer and not prosper. In contrast, the person who trusts the Lord will be blessed and lead a fruitful life. You can trust the God who is with you, cares for you, protects you, and is providentially bringing about his plan for your life. This will help you when you are tempted to fill your mind with fearful thoughts of what your abuser might do, or what might or might not happen if you were to behave in some way that would upset them too much.

Guilt

Does your abuser blame you for their own sin, failures and guilt and not just yours? If you accept the blame for these areas in their life, you will come to believe, as they already do, that if you had not said or done certain things, they would not have treated you in the way that they did. Since you are not the cause of their behavior, you are also not the solution for bringing about change in their thoughts, emotions, or behavior.

The importance of justification

It is really important that you understand the work of Jesus on the cross. The Bible teaches that you are by nature a sinner who deserves to be punished (Romans 3:10, 23) but through Jesus' death on the cross you have been made righteous before God (2 Corinthians 5:21; Romans 3:24 & 8:30). You are called to live on the basis of this righteous standing before God. Since you are in Christ, there is now no condemnation for you (Romans 8:1). You can reject this kind of condemning speech from your abuser because God has justified you, and Christ is seated at the right hand of God and is interceding for you (Romans 8:33, 34).

> Since you are not the cause of their behavior, you are also not the solution for bringing about change in their thoughts, emotions, or behavior

The role of sanctification

Being justified in Christ, you are to become like him in your character. This involves putting off the old self, renewing your thinking, and putting on the new self, created after the righteousness of God (Ephesians 4:22-24). If you are harboring, for example, anger, malice, strife, or jealousy in your heart (Colossians 3:8; Galatians 5:20; 1 Peter 2:1), it is important to understand that these belong to the old nature, and that you can repent of these heart attitudes.

Experiencing guilt for these things is the way that the Holy Spirit uses to bring about change in your life (John 16:8). Since God is *for* you in Christ, if you confess these sinful heart attitudes, you will be forgiven by him. He is your Advocate with the Father who is faithful and just (1 John 1:9-2:3).

At the same time, you should not accept condemnation from your abuser since Jesus died to take away your condemnation and is for you. By repenting of your personal sin, guilt is removed from your life. If you accept their accusations or insinuations as being true, or take the blame for their mistreatment of you, you will live in guilt. The reason for this is because you are not the cause of their behavior.

Anger

People in emotionally abusive relationships often struggle with anger. Anger is "a response by the whole person of negative moral judgment against perceived evil."31 Although the temptation to anger is a reaction to the way that your abuser treats you, any *sinful* anger on your part comes from out of your own heart. It involves both mental judgment of perceived evil and an emotional response *to* that evil.

The anger of God

Not all anger is sinful. We read in the Bible that God can be angry and exercise judgment. For example, he was angry with Moses when he asked that someone else lead Israel out of Egypt instead of him (Exodus 4:13-14). The psalmist warns against making the Son angry (Psalm 2:12). Jesus was angry when he saw people making a profit at the temple instead of it being a place of worship (John 2:13-17). His anger was due to the sin of the people.

Human righteous anger

People can also experience righteous anger. This is due to a sense of justice that people have because they are made in the image of a just God. When we see injustice, we want to see justice served. However, in order for anger to be righteous, it must involve the following: (1) a sin that has occurred; (2) a concern for the glory of God, not one's own glory; and (3) a righteous expression of that anger. For example, talking to the person who provoked you to anger about what happened in a way that addresses the issues involved, seeks mutual understanding, and does not attack the other person.

Human sinful anger

Human anger is usually sinful, and flows out of our heart, which is naturally corrupt. James 4:1-3 teaches that anger (part of fighting and quarreling) comes from thwarted desires: we cannot get what we want. Even asking God for it can fail if our motives are all wrong. The underlying attitude of the angry person is that they want something, desire, *covet* something, or are convinced that they deserve something. The angry person wants something so much that they are willing to sin in order to get it, and if they can't have it, they end up fighting and arguing with others. Anger is part of a sinful response to not getting what one desires or longs for (James 1:13-15).

Dealing with your angry heart

Any anger you experience comes from your own heart. Understanding this and working on what is going on in your heart will mean that you can live differently in your situation. We are called to conquer our anger (Proverbs 16:32, 22:24-25 & 25:28; Ephesians 4:31-32; James 1:19). Gaining insight into exactly what it is that you desire so much will help you deal with your anger.

You can discover this by asking a few questions:

- What circumstances led to my becoming angry?
- What did I say and do when I became angry?
- What did I say to myself when I became angry?
- What do I want from other people?

You may desire to be respected and not ordered around; to be shown love; for the abuser to be less angry at you; for the abuser to control their speech; for the abuser to acknowledge wrongdoing; or for the abuser to have fewer mood swings.

Change comes as you admit that these desires, which may be good in themselves, have actually been controlling you. This is extremely difficult to do, although possible with the Lord's enabling. After answering the questions above, you will probably see patterns when you become angry. For example, you might become angry when you see your abuser speaking to other people in a respectful way. You will also see that your thoughts go beyond the incident itself to thinking angrily about them and maybe the others involved. The answers will show you how you typically express your anger in what you say and do. From here you can plan ahead about what to think when you are in similar situations in the future. It is very helpful to think about truths in Scripture. 1 Peter is full of truths for people who are suffering at the hands of others. While filling your mind with biblical truths, you could find ways of regaining self-control so that you are not expressing your anger in wrong or sinful ways. An example is exercising, such as going for a walk or using an indoor bike.

Shame

A person experiences shame as a result of thinking that he or she is a failure. If you are experiencing shame, it could be because you believe that you are unable to live up to your abuser's standards – you believe that there is something wrong with you.

Since the shame is due to some kind of perceived failure on your part, you will never be able to achieve the desired standards they have for you – you believe that by nature you are inadequate. Your shame can also be due to your own behavior, something that was done to you by other people, or something about you which your abuser believes makes you inferior to them.

Shame in the Bible

We first see shame in the Bible in Genesis 3:7 when Adam and Eve covered themselves because they were naked. This is in contrast to Genesis 2:25 when Adam and Eve experienced no shame about being naked during the period of innocence before the fall in Genesis 3. The human experience of shame is a result of the guilt of sinning against God. The shame of nakedness is seen again in 2 Samuel 10:4, when Hanun shamed David's men by cutting off their clothes at the buttocks and shaving off half of each man's beard. In this case, the shame experienced was a result of a deliberate attempt by Hanun to humiliate David's men.

Christ removes shame

Christ is the answer for the shamed person. In the gospels we see that Jesus associated with those who were shamed by others because they were seen to be inferior. Examples are the woman at the well (John 4:1-45) and the tax collectors and other sinners (Matthew 9:9-13).

By dying on the cross, Jesus died in a shameful way, being naked and exposed to everybody who was looking at him. He fulfilled Isaiah 53:3-5, knowing the shame of being, "as one from whom men hide their faces, he was despised, and we esteemed him not." Even though he was innocent, he suffered shame so that others would be made righteous. Through his death and resurrection on the cross, Jesus canceled the debt that was against you and me (Colossians 2:14). As a result of his death on the cross when he became sin, you and I have become the righteousness of God (2 Corinthians 5:21). We have been justified by faith through Christ (Romans 5:1). There is now no condemnation for anyone in Christ Jesus! We are to live according to God's plan for our lives, being holy and blameless before him (Romans 8:1; Ephesians 1:4).

Righteous

You are righteous in Christ because of his work on the cross. Your shame has been borne by him so that you can live a godly life. Your alienation from God has been removed by Jesus so that you may be holy and blameless before him (Colossians 1:21-22).

Instead of accepting your abuser's judgment of you, look to how Jesus sees you. By nature, you are a sinner who does not match God's perfect standard and are cut off from him. But as a believer, you have been clothed with the righteousness of Christ because of his work on the cross. You belong to Christ, even if your abuser rejects and excludes you! Jesus has removed your shame in a personal, intimate way. In Isaiah 54:4-6 the Lord comforts Israel by saying that she is to forget her shame as he, her Maker, is her husband. This is true of the Church, the bride of Christ (Revelation 21:1-4). And you are part of the bride of Christ, in him you are holy and without blemish (Ephesians 5:27).

Jesus is the answer for the shamed person

Loneliness

Loneliness is an emotionally painful sense of not being connected to others. If you are feeling lonely, it may involve feelings of being unwanted, isolated, and left out. Your loneliness may be the result of living in fear, being isolated from others, a lack of intimacy with God, a lack of emotional connection with others, and a sense of being rejected by your abuser.

Examples of loneliness in the Bible

There are many examples of lonely people in the Bible. In 1 Kings 19:10 Elijah was in a state of great distress. He believed that he was the only one left alive who served the Lord. We also see in Scripture where David's soul waited in silence for God alone; he knew that the Lord was his only hope (Psalm 62:5). There was no other person who took notice of him or took care of his soul (Psalm 142:4). Asaph had no one on earth or heaven besides God (Psalm 73:25, 26). Demas, Crescens, and Titus left Paul; it was only the Lord who stood by him during his first trial (2 Timothy 4:10 & 16-17). Those closest to Jesus deserted him (Mark 14:50), Peter denied him (John 18:15-18; 25-27), and Judas betrayed him (Matthew 26:47-50). He was alone during his suffering in the Garden of Gethsemane (Matthew 26:36-46) and was forsaken by the Father when he hung on the cross (Matthew 27:46).

Dealing with loneliness

It is important to be connected to others. God has promised believers throughout the ages that he will neither leave them nor forsake them; he will always be with them (Psalm 139:7-12; Isaiah 41:10; Matthew 28:20; Hebrews 13:5). You can experience intimacy by knowing God as the Father of all compassion and the God of all comfort (2 Corinthians 1:3-4).

Christ is also your husband. What is meant by this? God compared his people in the Old Testament to a young wife who is deserted and grieved in spirit, a young woman rejected by her husband (Isaiah 54:5, 6). We read in Hosea that despite this, God betrothed his people to him in righteousness, justice, steadfast love, mercy, and faithfulness (Hosea 2:19, 20). Believers continue to be described as the bride of Christ in the New Testament (Ephesians 5:31-32; Revelation 21:2).

To overcome loneliness, it will also be important to establish relationships with other people. This will probably displease your abuser since coming out of your isolation will result in them having less control over you. This calls for wisdom about who you spend time with, and when.

Depression

If you are experiencing depression, you will probably believe that nothing in life has any sense or purpose. You may start to think that doing anything is pointless. You may find getting out of bed in the morning difficult. You may lack hope, think negatively, and see the worst in situations and people.

Dealing with your heart of depression

Perhaps your loss of hope is linked to your abuser not giving the love, respect, acceptance, and the kindness that you long for and expected. And this may be despite years of adapting and living according to their standards, views, and desires. It could be that these desires and your attempts to win their love and trust has superseded the place of the Lord in your life.

Knowing Jesus as the purpose in life

You have life-giving hope because, in Christ, you have received everything that you need to live in a godly way (2 Peter 1:3-4). It is possible to regain hope in life because you know that the God of hope desires that you live in hope, and that he can use your suffering for good (Romans 15:4; 5:1-5).

> **You belong to Jesus, even if your abuser rejects and excludes you**

It is important to think about what is true and to focus on the Lord. You will find it helpful to write down things that you can think about when you are tempted to think sad thoughts. You can ask your Christian friends to help you think according to who God is, what he has done for you, and what he has promised. As you work on these things, begin working on your use of time, and start with doing *one* responsible thing every day. Later, you can move on to following a schedule for the whole week. This scheduling should include set times for getting up in the morning and going to bed at night, eating healthily, and exercising.

Mike and Amy's story

As Mike and Amy explored the Bible for answers, they discovered that how we respond to life comes from our hearts, which is the immaterial aspect of our lives, from which come our motives, desires, and ways of thinking. They better realized that victims respond from their hearts to the horrible abuse they are suffering. Mike and Amy looked again at their lists of common outcomes of abuse and clearly saw that the Bible shows how to work on each of these outcomes. That gave them a lot of hope that they would be able to provide lasting help for those they were seeking to care for.

9. A New and Different Lifestyle

CLAIRE SENSED THAT she had built up a large grudge against her husband, Dennis, because of the way he consistently insulted, mocked, and demeaned her. Her parents had taught her to not say anything, keep the peace, and be nice. But that did not solve her resentment and anger.

Recently, she learned about how the Lord could change her angry heart by his Spirit. While letting the Spirit change her heart, she wanted to learn what that could look like in how she related to Dennis as well. She wanted to understand how to respond to Dennis in what she said, how to respond to the ways he treated her, and how to relate to him.

Honoring Christ in the home

Speech

In Genesis 1, we read many times that God spoke creation into being. And he gave human beings the ability to speak, which Adam used when he named the animals in Genesis 2, and exclaimed, "bone of my bones and flesh of my flesh", when he was introduced to the woman.

Satan manipulated words, in this case God's, when he spoke to the woman and questioned if God really *did* say that she should not eat of any tree in the garden. He then went on to claim that Adam and Eve would be like God, knowing good and evil if they ate from the tree of the knowledge of good and evil. As a result of Adam and Eve's decision to listen to Satan and disobey God and eat from the tree, human speech is affected by sin. We immediately see this when Adam and Eve then blamed each other and God for their own behavior (Genesis 3:12-13).

Our speech should be for the glory of Christ and the good of the other person (Colossians 4:6; Ephesians 4:29). The language that we speak comes out of our hearts (Mark 7:20-23; Matthew 12:34). By letting the Lord work on your heart, you will be enabled to speak in an appropriate way to your abuser, which humanly speaking seems like an impossible thing to do.

If they verbally attack you, you could say to them that you want to communicate with them in a calm and productive way, not in an aggressive manner. You could ask them to stop speaking to you in an attacking way. If they continue to do so, you could repeat what you have just said and add that you will leave the room if they do not stop. If they refuse to stop verbally attacking you, you should leave the room. If they continue attacking you, you could even leave the house. It is important that you create physical distance. If you are discussing an issue with your abuser and they start to verbally attack, accuse or blame you, or divert the conversation onto something else, instead of being diverted, becoming defensive or retaliating, it is important to stick to the issue being discussed by repeating what you were talking about in a polite and calm way.

All believers are called to care for one another and to confront fellow believers who are sinning (Galatians 6:1; Matthew 18:15), so it is right for you to confront your abuser when they are sinning against you. Being passive and not confronting sin will make it easier for them to continue to mistreat you. By confronting them, you are truly helping them because you are addressing issues in their life that do not correspond to the character of Jesus.

Boundaries

Preventing your abuser from speaking to you in an emotionally abusive manner is a way of setting boundaries around how you allow them to treat you. This is not selfish self-protection because you are setting limits to ensure they are less able to treat you in a way that is according to the old nature (Colossians 3:5-12; Galatians 5:19-21). You are helping them by seeking to prevent them from engaging in ungodly behavior. At the same time, you are seeking to think and behave in ways that honor the Lord.

If they counter your ideas or feelings, it is important *not* to try to explain or attempt to get them to understand you. In my long experience in counseling women in these sorts of situations, what will likely happen is that they will just counter your explanation and argue back at you. You should simply repeat what you said. If they discount what you say, you can say that you want your communication to honor the Lord.

Emotional abusers often make comments by joking. If they speak in this way, you should *not* explain why you don't think the joke was funny, because they will probably argue with you about your reasons, say that those reasons are foolish, and claim that you need to loosen up or that there is something wrong with you. When they deny that they have said certain things or treated you in a certain way, do not try to explain to them what happened in an attempt to make them remember or understand. Why? They probably *do* understand and know what happened.

> **Emotional abusers often make comments by joking**

Also, if you believe them when they deny things or counter you, you will probably begin to question your ability to perceive events and circumstances. In other words, don't get into an argument or long discussion as it will not help you, or them.

Doing good

Another way of honoring the Lord is in how you respond to your abuser. An important motivating desire is to avoid being overcome by evil, but to overcome evil with good (Romans 12:21). If you deal with the issues of your own heart, it will help ensure that you are not overcome by evil. By doing good toward your abuser, you are overcoming his evil with good.

Peter teaches this in 1 Peter 3:8-17. Instead of responding to evil with evil, put downs with put downs, and insults with insults, you should seek to bless them. This is only possible by the grace of God and the power of the Holy Spirit. In this way you will experience the Lord's blessing in your life. Good deeds include doing your daily tasks and seeking to be a blessing to others.

Mike and Amy's story

Seeing that victims of emotional abuse respond from the heart had given Mike and Amy much hope and insight into how to care for people. They then took this further and discovered the answers in the Bible about ways of speaking to abusive people, the importance of setting limits (or boundaries) to the sinful ways abusers treat them, and started to think what it would look like if victims responded by doing good and not going along with the abuse.

10. The Church as a Caring Community

TIM WAS CONCERNED about the malicious way Hannah treated her sister Sue. To help ensure that she had plenty of support, he introduced Sue to some of the other women after church one Sunday. They invited Sue to join their group and included her in social activities. Over time, they helped her learn how to respond to Hannah and supported her through any vengeful repercussions. As Sue listened to the church's teaching, she came to understand how the Lord sees her and learned to live in the light of that, instead of believing what Hannah had repeatedly told her.

It is important for you to be involved in a local church. As a Christian you are part of the people of God (Ephesians 2:11-22). You need other people in the Church to help you become a mature Christian, especially teachers and shepherds who provide this kind of help (Ephesians 4:11-14).

Church is important for you because you will hear teaching about the Lord, how to think truthfully, and how to live. This teaching should help you grow spiritually in your situation. For example, if you are taught that you are justified in Christ (Romans 5:1), no longer condemned because you are in him (Romans 8:1), and that no condemnation or charge against you will stand (Romans 8:33-34), you will be better able to reject accusatory and condemning words from your abuser. While it is essential that you have contact with other believers, it is important that you talk to your church leadership if your abuser is trying to control who you see. They can support you and give you advice about what to do in your situation.

Having other people in your life who can teach you how to deal with any negative thoughts you may have, will help you live as the Bible teaches rather than come under the control of your abuser. Being in relationship with other people will also prevent isolation, which will help stop your abuser controlling you. This is especially true if there are people in the Church who know about your situation, who believe you and *in* you, and do not take his good behavior in public at face value.

As the church provides care for victims, there are a number of practical ways that they can help. They could research and discover what the legal issues are in each situation and provide help if needed. They could help with child care, care of older people, and care of people with disabilities if needed. In many cases, it might be appropriate to help financially. It would be advisable for the church to consult with an advisory safeguarding body as they will be able to give advice and provide them with other resources.

Mike and Amy's story

Having discovered in the Bible about how abuse victims can change as they let the Lord work on their hearts, Mike and Amy were then struck by something else that the Bible teaches about change: it happens in community. Nobody can change on their own, and certainly not abuse victims. They need the church because they are spiritually born into the people of God. It helps them mature as believers, receive practical teaching about how to live, learn to think according to the Bible regarding their view of themselves, life, what is happening to them; and how to relate to the abuser, and to other people. Furthermore, Mike and Amy saw that the church needed to be informed about legal issues regarding abuse and have ways of providing practical care. This could include babysitting, legal advice regarding abuse and family law, care for an older person, or care for someone with a disability.

Closing Thoughts

THIS BOOK HAS looked at the mindset involved in emotional abuse, how this is expressed in the way abusive people relate to their victims, and how victims typically respond to the abusive person. It also explored who people are in Christ, how the Spirit can change the victim's heart and ways of relating, and the importance of the church.

It has explained what emotional abuse can look like in a spectrum of relationships and ministry contexts. Hopefully it has helped you gain more understanding of the dynamics of emotional abuse and that there are answers in the Bible. Since this is a short book, it is not possible to look at these issues in an in-depth way, so I would like to encourage you to continue on from what you have discovered here.

If you are interested in free resources about helping people, the *Center for Biblical Counseling and Discipleship* has a whole range of them on diverse topics.[7] *Conversations for Change* has practical resources and links to organizations that offer help.[8] If you would like to

7 The Center for Biblical Counseling & Discipleship: https://thecbcd.org/all-resources
8 Conversations for Change: https://biblicalcounsellingresources.com/

learn more about biblical soul care, *The Association of Certified Biblical Counselors* has a list of training centers that can provide this instruction.[9]

Emotional abuse causes tremendous suffering in victims' lives. May you be blessed as you compassionately care for the victims and seek to lead them to love and life in the Lord Jesus.

9 The Association of Certified Biblical Counselors: https://biblicalcounseling.com/training/

Bibliography

Note _____. *means same author as the one immediately before*

Barthel, Tara & David Edling. *Redeeming Church Conflicts: Turning Crisis into Compassion & Care.* Ada: Baker Books, 2012.

Bates, Liz. *Research summary on male victims of domestic abuse.* University of Cumbria. https://www.mankind.org.uk/wp-content/uploads/2021/11/ManKind-Conference-2021.pdf

Berkhof, Louis. *Systematic Theology.* Carlisle: Banner of Truth, 1996.

Berkouwer, G.C. *Studies in Dogmatics: Sin.* Grand Rapids: Eerdmans Publishing, 1980.

Caffaro, John. *Sibling Abuse of Other Children.* In: Geffner, R., White, J.W., Hamberger, L.K., Rosenbaum, A., Vaughan-Eden, V., Vieth, V.I. (eds) Handbook of Interpersonal Violence and Abuse Across the Lifespan. Springer, Cham.

DeGroat, Chuck. & Richard Mouw. *When Narcissism Comes to Church: Healing Your Community from Emotional & Spiritual Abuse.* IVP 2022.

Diggens, Mona. *Narcissistic Sibling: How to Recognize, Disarm, & Shield Yourself from Narcissistic Brothers & Sisters.* Bco Publishing, 2021.

Dryburgh, Anne. *The Emotionally Abusive Husband: Its Effects & How to Overcome Them in Christ.* Illumine Press, 2022.

_____. *The Emotionally Abusive Parent: Its Effects & How to Overcome Them in Christ.* Illumine Press, 2022.

Farmer, Steven. *Adult Children of Abusive Parents: A Healing Program for those who have Been Physically, Sexually, or Emotionally Abused.* Fort Wayne: Earth Magic Books, 2015.

Forward, Susan. *Mothers Who Can't Love: A Healing Guide for Daughters.* New York: HarperCollins, 2013.

Gemeay, Essmat Mohamed.? and Manal Mohamed El Kayal. *Impact of Elderly Abuse on Their Life Satisfaction.* Journal of US-China Medical Science, ISSN 1548-6648, USA, Mar. 2011, Volume 8, No. 3 (Serial No. 76), pp. 167-174.

Goggin, Jamin., & Kyle Strobel. *The Way of the Dragon & The Way of the Lamb: Searching for Jesus' Path for Power in a World that Has Abandoned It.* Thomas Nelson, 2021.

Golomb, Elan. *Trapped in the Mirror: Adult Children of Narcissists in their Struggle for Self.* New York: William Morrow and Company Inc, 1992.

Greydanus, Donald., Suzanne M. Greydanus-Rutgers and Joav Merrick. *Sibling abuse: a Cadmean victory for societal indifference*. Int J Adolesc Med Health 2016

Grossman, Frances, Joseph Spinazzola, Marla Zucker, & Elizabeth Hopper. *Treating Adult Survivors of Childhood Emotional Abuse & Neglect: A New Framework*. American Journal of Orthopsychiatry, 2017, Vol. 87, No. 1, 86-93.

Grudem, Wayne. *Systematic Theology: An Introduction to Systematic Theology*. Grand Rapids: Zondervan Publishing, 1994.

Herman, Judith. *Trauma and Recovery: The Aftermath of Violence – From Domestic Abuse to Political Terror*. New York: Basic Books, 2015.

_____. "Complex PTSD: A Syndrome in Survivors of Prolonged and Repeated Trauma." *Journal of Traumatic Stress* Vol. 5. No. 3, 1992.

Hines, Denise and Kathleen Malley-Morrison. *Psychological Effects of Partner Abuse Against Men: A Neglected Research Area*. Psychology of Men & Masculinity 2001, Vol. 2, No. 2, p. 75-85.

Homer, Ann., C Gilleard. *Abuse of elderly people by their carers*. BMJ Volume 301 15 December 1990.

Honeysett, Marcus. Powerful Leaders?: When Church Leadership Goes Wrong & How to Prevent It. IVP 2022.

Hopper, Elizabeth, Frances Grossman, Joseph Spinazzola & Marla Zucker. *Treating Adult Survivors of Childhood Emotional Abuse and Neglect: Component-Based Psychotherapy.* New York: The Guilford Press, 2019.

Horwitz, Allan, Cathy Widom, Julie McLaughlin, Helene White. "The Impact of Childhood Abuse and Neglect on Adult Mental Health: A Prospective Study." *Journal of Health and Social Behavior* Jun 2001 42:2.

Hourglass, Safer Aging, Stopping Abuse. *Keeping You and Your Loved Ones Safe from Neglect.* https://wearehourglass.org/sites/default/files/inline-files/Neglect%20Leaflet%202021%20Web_2.pdf

_____., *Keeping You and Your Loved Ones Safe from Financial Abuse.* https://wearehourglass.org/sites/default/files/inline-files/Financial%20Abuse%20leaflet%202021%20web_1.pdf

_____., *Keeping You and Your Loved Ones Safe from Psychological Abuse.* https://wearehourglass.org/sites/default/files/inline-files/Psychological%20Abuse%20leaflet%202021%20web_1.pdf

Johnson, David., & Jeff VanVonderen. *The Subtle Power of Spiritual Abuse: Recognizing and Escaping Spiritual Manipulation & False Spiritual Authority Within the Church.* Ada: Bethany House Publishers, 2005.

Kiselica, Mark., and Mandy Morrill-Richards. Sibling Maltreatment: The Forgotten Abuse. American

Counseling Association. https://www.counseling.org/knowledge-center/ethics

Lambert, Heath. *A Theology of Biblical Counseling: The Doctrinal Foundations of Counseling Ministry.* Grand Rapids: Zondervan Publishing, 2016.

Lanius, Ruth, Eric Vermettern, Claire Pain. *The Impact of Early Life Trauma on Health and Disease: The Hidden Epidemic.* Cambridge: Cambridge University Press, 2010.

Longobardi, Claudio., Laura Badenes-Ribera. *Vulnerability to violence and abuse among people with disabilities.* Life Span and Disability XXI, 1 (2018).

Longman, Tremper III & David Garland. *The Expositor's Bible Commentary 12: Ephesians – Philemon.* Grand Rapids: Zondervan Academic, 2006.

MacMillan Harriet. "Childhood Abuse and Lifetime Psychopathology in a Community Sample." *Am J Psychiatry* 158:11 November 2001.

McBride, Karyl. *Will I Ever be Good Enough: Healing the Daughters of Narcissistic Mothers.* New York: Atria Paperback, 2008.

Macey, Diana. *Narcissistic Mothers and Covert Emotional Abuse.* Independently Published, 2017.

Merkle, Benjamin. *ESV Expository Commentary: Ephesians.* Wheaton: Crossway, 2018.

Morrigan, Danu. *You're Not Crazy – It's Your Mother.* London: Darton, Longman, and Todd Ltd, 2012.

Nosek, Margaret., Carol Howland, and Rosemary Hughes. *The Investigation of Abuse and Women with Disabilities: Going Beyond Assumptions.* Violence Against Women, April 2001.

Nosek, Margaret., Catherine Clubb Foley, Rosemary B. Hughes, and Carol A. Howland. *Vulnerabilities for Abuse Among Women with Disabilities.* Sexuality and Disability, Vol. 19, No. 3, Fall 2001.

Okumusoglu, Sultan. *A Neglected Kind of Abuse: Elder Abuse; Violence towards Elderly.* IOSR Journal Of Humanities And Social Science (IOSR-JHSS) Volume 22, Issue 8, Ver. V (August. 2017) pp 16-20.

Powers, Laurie., Mary Oschwald. *Violence and Abuse Against People with Disabilities: Experiences, Barriers, and Prevention Strategies.* Center on Self-Determination Oregon Institute on Disability and Development Oregon Health & Science University.

Powlison, David. *Safe & Sound: Standing Firm in Spiritual Battles,* Greensboro: New Growth Press, 2019.

Rice, Linda. *Parenting the Difficult Child: A Biblical Perspective on Reactive Attachment Disorder.* Seedsown Press, 2012.

Rusac, Silvia. *Elderly Abuse and Alcohol Consumption.* University of Zagreb, Faculty of Law, Department of Social Work, Zagreb, Croatia. Coll Antropol. 39 (2015) 4: 869–875.

Smith, David. *With Willful Intent: A Theology of Sin.* Eugene: Wipf and Stock Publishers, 2003.

Tracy. Stephen. *Mending the Soul: Understanding and Healing Abuse.* Grand Rapids: Zondervan, 2005.

Venning, Ralph. *The Sinfulness of Sin.* Carlisle: Banner of Truth Trust, 1965.

Young, Mary Ellen., Margaret A. Nosek, Carol Howland, Gall Chanpong, and Diana H. Rintala. *Prevalence of Abuse of Women with Physical Disabilities.* Arch Phys Med Rehabil Vol 78, December 1997.

Endnotes

Note: _____. means same author as the one immediately before

Chapter One

1   Linda Belleville, *Women Leaders and the Church* (Grand Rapids: Baker Books, 2000), 100; Wayne Grudem, "The Key Issues in the Manhood and Womanhood Controversy, And the Way Forward." In *Biblical Foundations for Manhood and Womanhood,* ed. Wayne Grudem (Wheaton: Crossway Books, 2002), 19; James Hurley, *Man and Women in Biblical Perspective* (Leicester: Inter-varsity Press, 2005), 31; George Knight, "The Family and the Church: How Should Biblical Manhood and Womanhood Work Out in Practice?" In *Recovering Biblical Manhood and Womanhood,* ed. John Piper and Wayne Grudem (Wheaton: Crossway Books, 1991), 353; Linda Belleville, "Women in Ministry: An Egalitarian Perspective." In *Two Views on Women in Ministry,* 26; Elyse Fitzpatrick, *Helper by Design: God's Perfect Plan for Women in Marriage* (Chicago: Moody Publishers, 2003), 19.

2   Linda Belleville, *Women Leaders and the Church,*
     97; Richard Hess, "Equality With and Without
     Innocence: Genesis 1-3." In *Discovering Biblical
     Equality: Complementarity Without Hierarchy,*
     ed. Ronald Pierce and Rebecca Groothuis
     (Downers Grove: Inter-varsity Press, 2005),
     79; Craig Blomberg, "Women in Ministry: A
     Complementarian Perspective." In *Two Views on
     Women in Ministry,* ed. James Beck and Linda
     Belleville (Grand Rapids: Zondervan, 2005), 128.

3   Hess, "Equality Without Innocence: Genesis 1-3,"
     In *Discovery Biblical Equality: Complementarity
     Without Hierarchy,* 81; Bill Arnold, *Genesis.
     The New Cambridge Bible Commentary* (New
     York: Cambridge University Press, 2009), 45;
     R Davidson, *Genesis 1-11. The Cambridge Bible
     Commentary on the New English Bible* (Cambridge
     University Press, 1973), 24; Clare Amos, *The Book
     of Genesis* (Werrington: Biddles Ltd., 2004), 11.

4   Lambert, Heath. *A Theology of Biblical Counseling:
     The Doctrinal Foundations of Counseling Ministry.*
     Grand Rapids: Zondervan, 2016.

Chapter Two

5   This definition is an expansion of Engel's definition
     in Beverly Engel, *The Emotionally Abusive
     Relationship: How to Stop Being Abused and How
     to Stop Abusing* (Hoboken: John Wiley & Sons
     Inc., 2002), 10. This definition is expanded here

to include the effect of emotional abuse on the victim.

6   Evan Stark, *Coercive Control: How Men Entrap Women in Personal Life* (. New York: Oxford University Press, 2007), 249.

7   Albert Ellis and Marcia Powers, *The Secret of Overcoming Verbal Abuse: Getting Off the Emotional Roller Coaster and Regaining Control of Your Life,* (Hollywood: Wilshire Book Company, 2000), 18.

Chapter Three

8   Lundy Bancroft, *Why Does he Do That?: Inside the Minds of Angry and Controlling Men,* 125.

9   Marti Loring, *Emotional Abuse, Emotional Abuse.* (San Francisco: Jossey-Bass Publishers, 1994), 39.

10   _____., 233.

11   Ellis and Powers, *The Secret of Overcoming Verbal Abuse: Getting Off the Emotional Roller Coaster and Regaining Control of Your Life,* 28; Loring, *Emotional Abuse,* 218; Evans, *The Verbally Abusive Relationship: How to Recognize it and How to Respond,* 73; Hirigoyen, *Stalking the Soul: Emotional Abuse and the Erosion of Identity,* 155; Miller, *No Visible Wounds: Identifying Nonphysical Abuse of Women by their Men,* 44; Jerome Pieters et al., "Emotional, Physical, and Sexual Abuse: The Experiences of Men and Women," *Institute for the*

Equality of Men and Women, http ://igvm-iefh. belgium.be. (Accessed November 10, 2014).

Chapter Five

12 Bates, Liz. *Research summary on male victims of domestic abuse*. University of Cumbria. https://www.mankind.org.uk/wp-content/ uploads/2021/11/ManKind-Conference-2021. pdf; Hines, Denise and Kathleen Malley-Morrison. *Psychological Effects of Partner Abuse Against Men: A Neglected Research Area*. Psychology of Men & Masculinity 2001, Vol. 2, No. 2, p. 75-85;

13 World Health Organization. *Aging.* https://www. who.int/health-topics/ageing#tab=tab_1 (Accessed June 25, 2022).

14 Canadian Network for the Prevention of Elder Abuse. *The Toronto Declaration for the Prevention of Elder Abuse* (accessed June 25, 2022).

15 Gemeay, Essmat Mohamed.? and Manal Mohamed El Kayal. *Impact of Elderly Abuse on Their Life Satisfaction.* Journal of US-China Medical Science, ISSN 1548-6648, USA, Mar. 2011, Volume 8, No. 3 (Serial No. 76), pp. 167-174; Homer, Ann., C Gilleard. *Abuse of elderly people by their carers.* BMJ Volume 301 15 December 1990; Hourglass, Safer Aging, Stopping Abuse. *Keeping You and Your Loved Ones Safe from Neglect*. https:// wearehourglass.org/sites/default/files/inline-files/ Neglect%20Leaflet%202021%20Web_2.pdf

_____., *Keeping You and Your Loved Ones Safe from Financial Abuse*. https://wearehourglass.org/sites/default/files/inline-files/Financial%20Abuse%20leaflet%202021%20web_1.pdf

_____., *Keeping You and Your Loved Ones Safe from Psychological Abuse*. https://wearehourglass.org/sites/default/files/inline-files/Psychological%20Abuse%20leaflet%202021%20web_1.pdf; Okumusoglu, Sultan. *A Neglected Kind of Abuse: Elder Abuse; Violence towards Elderly*. IOSR Journal Of Humanities And Social Science (IOSR-JHSS) Volume 22, Issue 8, Ver. V (August. 2017) PP 16-20; Rusac, Silvia. *Elderly Abuse and Alcohol Consumption*. University of Zagreb, Faculty of Law, Department of Social Work, Zagreb, Croatia. Coll Antropol. 39 (2015) 4: 869–875.

16   Danu Morrigan, You're Not Crazy – It's Your Mother (London: Darton, Longman, and Todd Ltd, 2012), p 38 (as with other cited sources, the author does not agree with or endorse all that the writer teaches).

17   Another strategy is what is known as DARVO, an acronym for Deny, Attack, Reverse, Victim and Offender. The perpetrator may Deny the behavior, Attack the individual doing the confronting, and Reverse the roles of Victim and Offender with the result that the perpetrator then becomes the victim role and victim the perpetrator. For more information see: https://medium.com/

narcissistic-abuse-rehab/how-narcissists-use-darvo-to-escape-accountability-f0cb48708010

18   Farmer, Steven. *Adult Children of Abusive Parents: A Healing Program for those who have Been Physically, Sexually, or Emotionally Abused.* Fort Wayne: Earth Magic Books, 2015; Forward, Susan. *Mothers Who Can't Love: A Healing Guide for Daughters.* New York: HarperCollins, 2013; Golomb, Elan. *Trapped in the Mirror: Adult Children of Narcissists in their Struggle for Self.* New York: William Morrow and Company Inc, 1992; Grossman, Frances, Joseph Spinazzola, Marla Zucker, & Elizabeth Hopper. *Treating Adult Survivors of Childhood Emotional Abuse & Neglect: A New Framework.* American Journal of Orthopsychiatry, 2017, Vol. 87, No. 1, 86-93; Hopper, Elizabeth, Frances Grossman, Joseph Spinazzola & Marla Zucker. *Treating Adult Survivors of Childhood Emotional Abuse and Neglect: Component-Based Psychotherapy.* New York: The Guilford Press, 2019; Horwitz, Allan, Cathy Widom, Julie McLaughlin, Helene White. "The Impact of Childhood Abuse and Neglect on Adult Mental Health: A Prospective Study." *Journal of Health and Social Behavior* Jun 2001 42:2; MacMillan Harriet. "Childhood Abuse and Lifetime Psychopathology in a Community Sample." *Am J Psychiatry* 158:11 November 2001; McBride, Karyl. *Will I Ever be Good Enough: Healing the Daughters of Narcissistic Mothers.*

New York: Atria Paperback, 2008; Macey, Diana. *Narcissistic Mothers and Covert Emotional Abuse.* Independently Published, 2017.

19 Caffaro, John. *Sibling Abuse of Other Children.* In: Geffner, R., White, J.W., Hamberger, L.K., Rosenbaum, A., Vaughan-Eden, V., Vieth, V.I. (eds) Handbook of Interpersonal Violence and Abuse Across the Lifespan. Springer, Cham. https://doi.org/10.1007/978-3-319-62122-7_11-1; Diggens, Mona. *Narcissistic Sibling: How to Recognize, Disarm, & Shield Yourself from Narcissistic Brothers & Sisters.* Bco Publishing, 2021; Greydanus, Donald., Suzanne M. Greydanus-Rutgers and Joav Merrick. *Sibling abuse: a Cadmean victory for societal indifference.* Int J Adolesc Med Health 2016.

20 Longobardi, Claudio., Laura Badenes-Ribera. *Vulnerability to violence and abuse among people with disabilities.* Life Span and Disability XXI, 1 (2018); Nosek, Margaret., Carol Howland, and Rosemary Hughes. *The Investigation of Abuse and Women with Disabilities: Going Beyond Assumptions.* Violence Against Women April 2001; Nosek, Margaret., Catherine Clubb Foley, Rosemary B. Hughes, and Carol A. Howland. *Vulnerabilities for Abuse Among Women with Disabilities.* Sexuality and Disability, Vol. 19, No. 3, Fall 2001; Powers, Laurie., Mary Oschwald. *Violence and Abuse Against People with Disabilities: Experiences, Barriers, and Prevention Strategies.*

Center on Self-Determination Oregon Institute on Disability and Development Oregon Health & Science University; Young, Mary Ellen., Margaret A. Nosek, Carol Howland, Gall Chanpong, and Diana H. Rintala. *Prevalence of Abuse of Women with Physical Disabilities*. Arch Phys Med Rehabil Vol 78, December 1997.

Chapter Six

21   Barthel, Tara & David Edling. *Redeeming Church Conflicts: Turning Crisis into Compassion & Care.* Ada: Baker Books, 2012: DeGroat, Chuck. & Richard Mouw. *When Narcissism Comes to Church: Healing Your Community from Emotional & Spiritual Abuse.* IVP 2022; Goggin, Jamin., & Kyle Strobel. *The Way of the Dragon & The Way of the Lamb: Searching for Jesus' Path for Power in a World that Has Abandoned It.* Thomas Nelson, 2021; Honeysett, Marcus. Powerful Leaders?: When Church Leadership Goes Wrong & How to Prevent It. IVP 2022; Johnson, David., & Jeff VanVonderen. *The Subtle Power of Spiritual Abuse: Recognizing and Escaping Spiritual Manipulation & False Spiritual Authority Within the Church.* Ada: Bethany House Publishers, 2005.

Chapter Eight

22   Edward Welch, *Blame it on the Brain: Distinguishing Chemical Imbalances, Brain*

Disorders, and Disobedience (Phillipsburg: P&R
Publishing, 1998), 35.

23 Leland Ryken, James Wilhoit, and Tremper
Longman, ed. *Dictionary of Biblical Imagery: An
encyclopedic exploration of the images, symbols,
motifs, metaphors, figures of speech and literary
patterns of the Bible* (Downers Grove: InterVarsity
Press, 1998), 368.

24 _____., 36; Howard Eyrich and William
Hines, *Curing the Heart: A Model for Biblical
Counseling* (Fearn: Christian Focus Publications
Ltd., 2002), 45.

25 _____., 45; Welch, *Blame it on the Brain:
Distinguishing Chemical Imbalances, Brain
Disorders, and Disobedience*, 36.

26 George Scipione, "Worry," *CCEF – West San Diego
92.* CD ibc9233.

27 Pryde and Needham, *A Biblical Perspective of What
to Do When You Are Abused By Your Husband,* 59.

28 Priolo, "Helping People Pleasers," *National
Association of Nouthetic Counselors.*

29 Wayne Grudem, *Systematic Theology: An
Introduction to Biblical Doctrine* (Leicester: Inter-
varsity Press, 1994), 96-97.

30 Welch, *When People Are Big and God is Small,* 96-97.

31 Jim Newheiser, "Anger/Abuse," *Institute for Biblical
Counseling & Discipleship.*

Printed in Great Britain
by Amazon